Darśan

Darśan

Seeing the Divine Image in

India

Second Revised and Enlarged Edition

Diana L. Eck

Columbia University Press
New York

Cover. Ardhanārīśvara, "Half-woman Lord" from Yiruvenkadu, Tanjore District.
Courtesy of the National Art Gallery, Madras

Frontispiece. Srīraṅgam, Ranganathaswami Temple, Tiruchirapalli, Tamilnādu, Fifteenth century.
© American Institute of Indian Studies, Banāras

Columbia University Press
Publishers Since 1893
New York Chichester, West Sussex

Columbia University Press edition, 1996

Library of Congress Cataloging-in-Publication Data
Eck, Diana L.
Darśan, seeing the divine image in India / Diana L. Eck.—2nd rev. and enl. ed.
p. cm.
Includes bibliographical references and index.
ISBN 0-231-10845-1 (pbk. : alk. paper)
1. Hinduism. 2. Hindu symbolism. I. Title.
BL1205.E25 1996
294.5—dc20 96-36343
CIP

∞

Printed in the United States of America
p 10 9 8 7 6 5 4 3 2 1

Foreword

THIS VOLUME is intended as an aid to our vision (*darśan*: seeing), and consequently it is full of ideas. To the extent that we allow ourselves to see from within the perspective (see through, thoroughly) of Professor Diana Eck, we will experience the intimate relationship, and necessary cooperation between, seeing and thinking, image and idea. In its emphasis on the interdependence of the visual and intellectual, this guide claims a uniquely important role for the visual (*darśan*) in the Hindu religious tradition.

Because of the essential role of the visual in the Indian tradition, our characteristic failure to make visual sense of Hindu images lands us in absurdities. Even intelligent and thoughtful viewers may fail to see (grasp, sympathetically understand) images as foreign as those which populate the Indian religious landscape. Professor Eck points to the sad example of Mark Twain, a brilliant interpreter of his own culture, who experienced Hindu images in the holy city of Banāras, only to dismiss them as "idols" — "crude, misshapen and ugly" (page 18). Those of us — whether professors, college students or independent learners — who wish to avoid Mark Twain's misperception which turns images of the divine into ugly idols would do well to see these images through Professor Eck's informed perspective. If we read, think, and look with tolerance and imagination (image-ing), we will see a world of religious meaning otherwise inaccessible to us. Such would be the intention, or invitation, of this guide: "This book is written as a companion for those who want to "see" something of India, in the hope that what catches the eye may change our minds" (Preface, page 2).

Just what are these images that Professor Eck invites us to see, and the ideas which might enable us to see their meanings? The key term of the title, *darśan*, indicates the guide's content and method. The entire guide concerns *darśan*, a Sanskrit word that means seeing, especially seeing the divine in an image, in a person or in a set of ideas. This guide concentrates on the first two of these meanings: the divine in sculpture, temples, symbols, times, and places, and the divine in great spiritual figures throughout the history of the Hindu religious tradition. The third meaning, the divine in ideas, is also important because it refers to our view of the world and of the divine. *Darśan* also refers to the six systems of philosophy based on the Veda, the ancient Indian scriptures. This meaning of *darśan* is important for our ability to see (i.e., understand) Hinduism because it is our worldview, our philosophy, which prevents us from seriously considering the Hindu claim that Śiva and Kṛṣṇa, and their images, truly contain or manifest the divine. So while Professor Eck is primarily concerned to show us images of the divine, she is also trying to show why we ordinarily fail to see their divinity — and if we do not see them as in any sense divine, then we have not seen them in their Hindu, or religious, meaning.

As with the word *darśan*, the words in the subtitle — "Seeing the Divine Image in India" — will become clearer, and more revealing, as we attempt to see from within the Hindu *darśan*. Creative seeing may replace our ordinary passive viewing (looking without insight, without informed perspective). Similarly, if we do the kind of seeing which could change our minds, we might eventually gain a glimpse of the divine in one of the myriad images of India's multitude of gods. Finally, in so doing, we would begin to understand the celebration of the divine not only in gods but also in persons, animals, rivers and rocks. It is this celebration of the divine in the world for which India has been the foremost exponent and exemplar for more than three millennia. So far from seeing ugly idols, we would then see with a vision which includes and advances understanding.

Darśan: Seeing the Divine Image in India first appeared as part of a series, "Focus on Hinduism and Buddhism," edited by Robert A. McDermott, which was supported by grants from the National Endowment for the Humanities to the Council on International and Public Affairs, Inc., the Ada Howe Kent Foundation, and Baruch College CUNY.

This revised and enlarged edition of Professor Eck's study of *Darśan* adds many more striking photographs to the earlier edition and presents her work in a more readable and attractive format.

Robert A. McDermott
Series Editor

Harry M. Buck
Publisher

Contents

Preface

IN A MEMORABLE episode in Hindu mythology, the great God Śiva and the Goddess Pārvatī are sporting in their high Himālayan home when Pārvatī, in play, covers Śiva's eyes with her hands. The whole universe is suddenly plunged into darkness. When Śiva's eyes are closed, there is no light anywhere, except the fire of Śiva's third eye, which threatens destruction. The all-seeing gods are said never to close their eyes, and from the near-disaster of Śiva and Pārvatī's play, it is clearly a good thing that they don't, for the well-being of the world is dependent on the open eyes of the Lord.

This is an essay about the power and importance of "seeing" in the Hindu religious tradition. In the Hindu view, not only must the gods keep their eyes open, but so must we, in order to make contact with them, to reap their blessings, and to know their secrets. When Hindus go to the temple, their eyes meet the powerful, eternal gaze of the eyes of God. It is called *darśan*, "seeing" the divine image, and it is the single most common and significant element of Hindu worship. Here we will explore what *darśan* means.

This is also an essay about the divine image in the Hindu tradition. We ask, and we are not the first to do so, "What do Hindus *see* in the images of the gods? What is meant by these multi-armed gods, with their various weapons, emblems, and animals? How are these images made and consecrated? How are they treated in a ritual context?" In exploring the nature of the divine image, we will not limit ourselves to the images of the gods as such, but we will consider the ways in which the Hindu temple and the Hindu place of pilgrimage have become "divine images" as well.

This study is based on the conviction that "seeing" is not only the goal and prerogative of the sages, the "seers," but it is part of all our learning and knowing. As teachers and students of a culture as visually oriented as that of India, we too must become "seers." Ideally, we would spend many months in India, traveling and reflecting on what we see. Given our limitations, however, we may bring something of the visual dimension of Indian culture into our study of

Hinduism in the works of art, the slides, and the films which serve as a starting point for study and discussion. Such things are not merely "visual aids" in a learning process which is primarily textual. We should rather see them as "visual texts" which, like the books on our syllabus, require discussion, interpretation, and perhaps "rereading." Help can be found in the volume *Focus on Hinduism* (Anima Books, 1981), one of two key books in the series of which this volume was originally a part.

Certainly in the case of Indian art and images, such visual texts present their own perspective on the "Hindu tradition," and one that is not simply an "illustration" of what can already be learned from the rich textual traditions of Sanskrit. For those who would know something of how Hindus understand their own tradition, what is "written" in India's images certainly demands the same kind of careful attention to content and interpretation as might be devoted to what is written in India's scriptural tradition.

It was in seeing India — its arts, images, and landscapes — that I first was drawn to the study of Hinduism and Sanskrit. And of the many things I continue to find fascinating about Hinduism, it is the Hindu imagination with its vibrant capacity for image-making which is still at the source of it all. This book is written as a companion for those who want to "see" something of India, in the hope that what catches the eye may change our minds.

Diana Eck

CHAPTER 1

Seeing the Sacred

A. Darśan

A COMMON SIGHT in India is a crowd of people gathered in the courtyard of a temple or at the doorway of a streetside shrine for the *darśan* of the deity. Darśan means "seeing." In the Hindu ritual tradition it refers especially to religious seeing, or the visual perception of the sacred. When Hindus go to a temple, they do not commonly say, "I am going to worship," but rather, "I am going for *darśan*." They go to "see" the image of the deity — be it Kṛṣṇa or Durgā, Śiva or Viṣṇu — present in the sanctum of the temple, and they go especially at those times of day when the image is most beautifully adorned with fresh flowers and when the curtain is drawn back so that the image is fully visible. The central act of Hindu worship, from the point of view of the lay person, is to stand in the presence of the deity and to behold the image with one's own eyes, to see and be seen by the deity. *Darśan* is sometimes translated as the "auspicious sight" of the divine, and its importance in the Hindu ritual complex reminds us that for Hindus "worship" is not only a matter of prayers and offerings and the devotional disposition of the heart. Since, in the Hindu understanding, the deity is present in the image, the visual apprehension of the image is charged with religious meaning. Beholding the image is an act of worship, and through the eyes one gains the blessings of the divine.

Similarly, when Hindus travel on pilgrimage, as they do by the millions each month of the year, it is for the *darśan* of the place of pilgrimage or for the *darśan* of its famous deities. They travel to Śiva's sacred city of Banāras for the *darśan* of Lord Viśvanāth. They trek high into the Himālayas for the *darśan* of Viṣṇu at Badrīnāth. Or they climb to the top of a hill in their own district

Munshi Ghāṭ, Banāras

for the *darśan* of a well-known local goddess. The pilgrims who take to the road on foot, or who crowd into buses and trains, are not merely sightseers, but "sacred sightseers" whose interest is not in the picturesque place, but in the powerful place where *darśan* may be had. These powerful places are called *tīrthas* (sacred "fords" or "crossings"), *dhāms* (divine "abodes"), or *pīṭhas* (the "benches" or "seats" of the divine). There are thousands of such places in India. Some, like Banāras (Vārāṇasī), which is also called Kāśī, are sought by pilgrims from their immediate locales.

Often such places of pilgrimage are famous for particular divine images, and so it is for the *darśan* of the image that pilgrims come. The close relationship between the symbolic importance of the image and the symbolic act of pilgrimage has been explored in a Western context by Victor and Edith Turner in *Image and Pilgrimage in Christian Culture*.[1] In the West, of course, such traditions of pilgrimage were often attacked by those who did not "see" the symbolic significance of images and who, like Erasmus, denounced the undertaking of pilgrimages as a waste of time. In the Hindu tradition, however, there has never been the confusion of "image" with "idol," and in India, pilgrimage is the natural extension of the desire for the *darśan* of the divine image, which is at the heart of all temple worship.

It is not only for the *darśan* of renowned images that Hindus have traveled as pilgrims. They also seek the *darśan* of the places themselves which are said to be the natural epiphanies of the divine: the peaks of the Himālayas, which are said to be the abode of the gods; the river Gaṅgā, which is said to fall from heaven to earth; or the many places which are associated with the mythic deeds of gods and goddesses, heroes and saints.

In addition to the *darśan* of temple images and sacred places, Hindus also value the *darśan* of holy persons, such as *sants* ("saints"), *sādhus* ("holy men"), and *sannyāsins* ("renouncers"). When Mahatma Gandhi traveled through India, tens of thousands of people would gather wherever he stopped in order to "take his *darśan*." Even if he did not stop, they would throng the train stations for a passing glimpse of the Mahatma in his compartment. Similarly, when Swami Karpātrī, a well-known *sannyāsin* who is also a writer and political leader, would come to Vārāṇasī to spend the rainy season "retreat" period, people would flock to his daily

Painter putting finishing touches on the silver cap of the liṅga of Mahākāla in Ujjaih

lectures not only to hear him, but to see him. However, even an ordinary *sannyāsin* or *sādhu* is held in esteem in traditional Hindu culture. He is a living symbol of the value placed upon renunciation, and he is a perpetual pilgrim who has left home and family for a homeless life. Villagers are eager for the *darśan* of such a person, approaching him with reverence and giving him food and hospitality. In *The Ochre Robe,* Agehananda Bharati writes, "There is absolutely no parallel to the conception of *darśan* in any religious act in the West. . . ."[2]

In popular terminology, Hindus say that the deity or the *sādhu* "gives *darśan*" (*darśan denā* is the Hindi expression), and the people "take *darśan*" (*darśan lenā*). What does this mean? What is given and what is taken? The very expression is arresting, for "seeing" in this religious sense is not an act which is initiated by the worshiper.[3] Rather, the deity presents itself to be seen in its image, or the *sādhu* gives himself to be seen by the villagers. And the people "receive" their *darśan*. One might say that this "sacred perception," which is the ability truly to see the divine image, is given to the devotee, just as Arjuna is given the eyes with which to see Kṛṣṇa in the theophany described in the Bhagavad Gītā.[4]

The prominence of the eyes of Hindu divine images also reminds us that it is not only the worshiper who sees the deity, but the deity sees the worshiper as well. The contact between devotee and deity is exchanged through the eyes. It is said in India that one of the ways in which the gods can be recognized when they move among people on this earth is by their unblinking eyes. Their gaze and their watchfulness is uninterrupted. Jan Gonda, in his detailed monograph *Eye and Gaze in the Veda*, has enumerated the many ways in which the powerful gaze of the gods was imagined and expressed even in a time before actual images of the gods were crafted.[5] The eyes of Sūrya or Agni or Varuṇa are powerful and all-seeing, and the gods were entreated to look upon men with a kindly eye.

In the later Hindu tradition, when divine images began to be made, the eyes were the final part of the anthropomorphic image to be carved or set in place. Even after the breath of life (*prāṇa*) was established in the image there was the ceremony in which the eyes were ritually opened with a golden needle or with the final stroke of a paintbrush. This is still common practice in the consecration of images, and today shiny oversized enamel eyes may be set in the eye-sockets of the image during this rite. The gaze which falls from the newly-opened eyes of the deity is said to be so powerful that it must first fall upon some pleasing offering, such as sweets, or upon a mirror where it may see its own reflection. More than once has the tale been told of that powerful gaze falling upon some unwitting bystander, who died instantly of its force.[6]

Hindu divine images are often striking for their large and conspicuous eyes. The famous image of Kṛṣṇa Jagannāth in Purī has enormous saucer-like eyes.[7] Śiva and Gaṇeśa are often depicted with a third vertical eye, set in the center of the forehead. Brahmā, inheriting the name "Thousand-Eyes" from Indra, is sometimes depicted with eyes all over his body, like leopard spots. While it would take us too far afield to explore the many dimensions of eye-power in the Hindu tradition, it is important for this study of the divine image to recognize that just as the glance of the inauspicious is thought to be dangerous and is referred to as the "evil eye," so is the glance of the auspicious person or the deity held to be profitable. When Hindus stand on tiptoe and crane their necks to see, through the crowd, the image of Lord Kṛṣṇa, they wish not only to "see," but to be seen. The gaze of the huge eyes of the image meets that of the worshiper, and that exchange of vision lies at the heart of Hindu worship.

Śiva on Temples at Koṇārak, Central North India

In the Indian context, seeing is a kind of touching. The art historian Stella Kramrisch writes,

> Seeing, according to Indian notions, is a going forth of the sight towards the object. Sight touches it and acquires its form. Touch is the ultimate connection by which the visible yields to being grasped. While the eye touches the object, the vitality that pulsates in it is communicated. . . .[8]

Examining the words used in the Vedic literature, Gonda reaches the same conclusion: "That a look was consciously regarded as a form of contact appears from the combination of 'looking' and 'touching.' Casting one's eyes upon a person and touching him were related activities."[9]

Sanskrit poets and dramatists convey the subtleties of meaning expressed by the glances of the eyes, not only between lovers, but between husband and wife, whose public conversation was limited by rules of propriety.[10] They communicated in their glances. Writes Daniel H. H. Ingalls, "One must suppose that the language of the eyes was more advanced in ancient India than it is with us."[11] Gonda reflects on the "language of the eyes" as it may pertain to the religious context: "It is indeed hardly conceivable that the psychical contact brought about, in normal social intercourse, by the eye, should not, consciously or unconsciously, have been made an element in a variety of rites and religious customs, that the positive fascination of a prolonged look, fixed regard or other manners of looking should not, in ritual practice also, be a means of expressing feelings, of imposing silence, of signifying consent or satisfaction, of expressing will, love or reverence, a means also of participating in the essence and nature of the person or object looked at."[12]

Not only is seeing a form of "touching," it is a form of knowing. According to the Brāhmaṇas, "The eye is the truth (*satyam*). If two persons were to come disputing with each other, . . . we should believe him who said 'I have seen it,' not him who has said 'I have heard it.'"[13] Seeing is not only an activity of the eye, however. In India, as in many cultures, words for seeing have included within their semantic fields the notion of knowing. We speak of "seeing" the point of an argument, of "insight" into an issue of complexity, of the "vision" of people of wisdom. In Vedic India the "seers" were called *ṛṣis*. In their hymns, collected in the Ṛg Veda, "to see" often means a "mystical, supranatural beholding" or "visionary experiencing."[14] Later on, the term *darśana* was used to describe the systems of philosophy which developed in the Indian tradition. However, it is misleading to think of these as "systems" or "schools" of philosophical thought. Rather, they are "points of view" which represent the varied phases of the truth viewed from different angles of vision."[15]

B. The Visible India

Hinduism is an imaginative, an "image-making," religious tradition in which the sacred is seen as present in the visible world — the world we see in multiple images and deities, in sacred places, and in people. The notion of *darśan* calls our attention, as students of Hinduism, to the fact that India is a visual and visionary culture, one in which the eyes have a prominent role in the apprehension of the sacred. For most ordinary Hindus, the notion of the divine as "invisible" would be foreign indeed. God is eminently visible, although human beings have not always had the refinement of sight to see. Furthermore, the divine is visible not only in temple and shrine, but also in the whole continuum of life — in nature, in people, in birth and growth and death. Although some Hindus, both philosophers and radical reformers, have always used the terms *nirguṇa* ("qualityless") and *nirākāra* ("formless") to speak of the One Brahman, this can most accurately be understood only from the perspective of a tradition that has simultaneously affirmed that Brahman is also *saguṇa* ("with qualities"), and that the multitude of "names and forms" of this world are the exuberant transformations of the One Brahman.

India presents to the visitor an overwhelmingly visual impression. It is beautiful, colorful, sensuous. It is captivating and intriguing, repugnant and puzzling. It combines the intimacy and familiarity of English four o'clock tea with the dazzling foreignness of carpisoned elephants or vast crowds bathing in the Gaṅgā during an eclipse. India's display of multi-armed images, its processions and pilgrimages, its beggars and kings, its street life and markets, its diversity of peoples — all appear to the eye in a kaleidoscope of images. Much that is removed from public view in the modern

West and taken into the privacy of rest homes, asylums, and institutions is open and visible in the life of an Indian city or village. The elderly, the infirm, the dead awaiting cremation — these sights, while they may have been expunged from the childhood palace of the Buddha, are not isolated from the public eye in India. Rather, they are present daily in the visible world in which Hindus, and those who visit India, move in the course of ordinary activities. In India, one sees everything. One sees people at work and at prayer; one sees plump, well-endowed merchants, simple renouncers, fraudulent "holy" men, frail widows, and emaciated lepers; one sees the festival procession, the marriage procession, and the funeral procession. Whatever Hindus affirm of the meaning of life, death, and suffering, they affirm with their eyes wide open.

So abundant are the data of the visual India, seen with the eye, that what one has learned from reading about "Hinduism" may seem pale and perhaps unrecognizable by comparison. As E. M. Forster wrote of the enterprise of studying Hinduism: "Study it for years with the best of teachers, and when you raise your head, nothing they have told you quite fits."[16]

The medium of film is especially important for the student of Hinduism, for it provides a way of entering the visual world, the world of sense and image, which is so important for the Hindu tradition. Raising the eye from the printed page to the street or the temple, as conveyed by the film, provides a new range of questions, a new set of data. In India's own terms, seeing is knowing. And India must be seen to be known. While Hindu spirituality is often portrayed in the West as interior, mystical, and other-worldly, one need only raise the head from the book to the image to see how mistakenly one-sided such a characterization is. The day to day life and ritual of Hindus is based not upon abstract interior truths, but upon the charged, concrete, and particular appearances of the divine in the substance of the material world.

Many Westerners, for example, upon seeing Hindu ritual observances for the first time, are impressed with how sensuous Hindu worship is. It is sensuous in that it makes full use of the senses — seeing, touching, smelling, tasting, and hearing. One "sees" the image of the deity (*darśan*). One "touches" it with one's hands (*sparśa*), and one also "touches" the limbs of one's own body to establish the presence of various deities (*nyāsa*). One "hears"

Pouring water through a ritual implement upon the four-faced silver crown of Śiva. By the tank of the River Godāvarī in Nāsik

the sacred sound of the *mantras* (*śravaṇa*). The ringing of bells, the offering of oil lamps, the presentation of flowers, the pouring of water and milk, the sipping of sanctified liquid offerings, the eating of consecrated food — these are the basic constituents of Hindu worship, *pūjā*. For all of its famous otherworldliness, India is a culture that has also celebrated the life of this world and the realms of the senses.

C. Film Images

What do we mean by *image*? The term has been used variously in psychology, philosophy, religion, and the arts. For our purposes, there are two ways in which *image* is being used. First, there are the artistic images, the "icons" of the Hindu religious tradition, which are a primary focus of this essay. The creation of such images is perhaps the earliest form of human symbolization. People lifted out of the ordinary visible data of the world a shape, a form, which crystallized experience and, with its meanings and connotations, told a story. Long before people wrote textual treatises, they "wrote" in images. The term iconography means, literally, "writing in images." These visual texts, such as the great temples of

Khajurāho or Koṇārak or the array of icons within a modern Hindu temple, constitute a considerable heritage of the human imagination for the scholar of religion. One must learn to "read" these visual texts with the same insight and interpretive skill that is brought to the reading and interpretation of scriptures, commentaries, and theologies.

Here, however, we are concerned with a second meaning of the term *image* — the visual images of India that are presented to us through the medium of film and photography. Rudolf Arnheim has noted what he calls the "widespread unemployment of the senses in every field of academic study."[17] Photographic images enable us to employ the senses in the process of learning. But they also give us pause to reflect on the role of this new, almost "magical," form of image-making in our own culture and in our efforts to know and understand another culture.

Munshi Ghāṭ, Banāras

Photography and film have made possible the mass proliferation of images. In *On Photography*, Susan Sontag has reflected on the ways in which photography has become a way of defining, appropriating, and recycling "reality."[18] The image business has become an important part of modern consumerism and has turned all of us into the creators and consumers of images. People take photographs, buy photographs, go to films, watch television, glance at billboard advertisements. In short, photography has "greatly enlarged the realm of the visible."[19] Both Sontag's articulation and critique of the prominence of the image in modern society serve to underline our need to think seriously about the interpretation and use of film images. We can "see" such scenes as the Hindu pilgrims bathing in the River Gaṅgā in Banāras or the Muslim mourners beating their chests with their fists. But what do we "make" of what we see? Seeing, after all, is an imaginative, constructive activity, an act of making. It is not simply the reception of images on the retina.

The term *hermeneutics* has been used to describe the task of understanding and interpreting ideas and texts. In a similar way, we need to set for ourselves the task of developing a hermeneutic of the visible, addressing the problem of how we understand and interpret what we see, not only in the classical images and art forms created by the various religious traditions, but in the ordinary images of people's traditions, rites, and daily activities which are presented to us through the film-image.

Rudolf Arnheim, in his extensive work on visual perception, has shown that the dichotomy between seeing and thinking which runs through much of the Western tradition, is a very problematic one. In *Visual Thinking*, he contends that visual perception is integrally related to thought.[20] It is not the case, according to Arnheim, that the eyes present a kind of raw data to the mind which, in turn, processes it and refines it by thought. Rather, those visual images are the shapers and bearers of thought. Jan Gonda, in writing on the Vedic notion *dhi-*, sometimes translated as "thought," finds similarly that the semantic field of this word in Vedic literature does not correspond as much to our words for "thinking" as it does to our notions of "insight," "vision," and "seeing."[21] Susanne Langer has also written of the integral relation of thought to the images we see in the "mind's eye." The making of all those images is the fundamental "imaginative" human activity. One might add that it is the fundamental activity of the religious imagination as well. She writes, "Images are, therefore, our readiest instruments for abstracting concepts from the tumbling streams of actual impressions."[22]

Seeing is not a passive awareness of visual data, but an active focusing upon it, "touching" it. Arnheim writes, in language that echoes the Hindu notion of seeing and touching: "In looking at an object we reach out for it. With an invisible finger we move through the space around us, go out to the distant places where things are found, touch them, catch them, scan their surfaces, trace their borders, explore their texture. It is an eminently active occupation."[23]

According to Arnheim, the way in which we reach out for and grasp the "object we see, either in our immediate range of perception or through the medium of photography, is dependent upon who we are and what we recognize from past experience." The visual imprint of an image, an object, or a scene upon the eye is not at all "objective." In the image-making process of thinking, we see, sort, and recognize according to the visual phenomenology of our own experience.[24] What people notice in the "same" image — be it an image of the dancing Śiva or a film of a Hindu festival procession — depends to some extent on what they can recognize from the visual experience of the past. In the case of film, of course, it also depends on what the photographer has seen and chosen to show us. Arnheim writes that the eye and the mind, working together in the process of cognition, cannot simply note down images that are "already there." "We find instead that direct observation, far from being a mere ragpicker, is an exploration of the form-seeking, form-imposing mind, which needs to understand but cannot until it casts what it sees into manageable models."[25]

As students confronted with images of India through film and photography, we are challenged to begin to be self-conscious of who we are as "seers." Part of the difficulty of entering the world of another culture, especially one with as intricate and elaborate a visual articulation as India's, is that, for many of us, there are no "manageable models." There are no self-evident ways of recognizing the shapes and forms of art, iconography, ritual life and daily life that we see. Who is Śiva, dancing wildly in a ring of fire? What is happening when the priest pours honey and yogurt over the image of Viṣṇu? Why does the woman touch the feet of the ascetic beggar? For those who enter the visible world of India through the medium of film, the onslaught of strange images raises a multitude of questions. These very questions should be the starting point for our learning. Without such self-conscious questioning, we cannot begin to "think" with what we see and we simply dismiss it as strange. Or, worse, we are bound to misinterpret what we see by placing it solely within the context of what we already know from our own world of experience.

It has sometimes been claimed that the photograph is a kind of universal "language," but our reflections here make us question such a claim. Every photograph and film raises the question of point-of-view and perspective — both that of the maker and that of the viewer. And it raises the question of meaning. This "language," like speech, can obstruct as well as facilitate communication and understanding. Sontag writes that if a photograph is supposed to be a "piece of the world," we need to know *what* piece of the world it is.[26] We need to inquire after its context. She cites Harold Edgerton's famous photograph of what appears to be a coronet, but is really a splash of milk, and Weston's photograph of what appears to be gathered cloth, but is a close-up of a cabbage-leaf. A picture, such as that of a brahmin priest decorating a Śiva *liṅga* for the evening *āratī*, or that of the Goddess Durgā standing upon Mahiṣa may be worth a thousand words, but still we need to know which thousand words.

D. The Image of God

The vivid variety of Hindu deities is visible everywhere in India. Rural India is filled with countless wayside shrines. In every town of some size there are many temples, and every major temple will contain its own panoply of shrines and images. One can see the silver mask of the goddess Durgā, or the stone shaft of the Śiva *liṅga*, or the four-armed form of the god Viṣṇu. Over the doorway of a temple or a home sits the plump, orange, elephant-headed Gaṇeśa or the benign and auspicious Lakṣmī. Moreover, it is not only in temples and homes that one sees the images of the deities. Small icons are mounted at the front of taxis and buses. They decorate the walls of tea stalls, sweet shops, tailors, and movie theatres. They are painted on public buildings and homes by local folk artists. They are carried through the streets in great festival processions.

Śiva Liṅga

It is visibly apparent to anyone who visits India or who sees something of India through the medium of film that this is a culture in which the mythic imagination has been very generative. The images and myths of the Hindu imagination constitute a basic cultural vocabulary and a common idiom of discourse. Since India has "written" prolifically in its images, learning to read its mythology and iconography is a primary task for the student of Hinduism. In learning about Hinduism, it might be argued that perhaps it makes more sense to begin with Gaṇeśa, the elephant-headed god who sits at the thresholds of space and time and who blesses all beginnings, and then proceed through the deities of the Hindu pantheon, rather than to begin with the Indus Valley civilization and proceed through the ages of Hindu history. Certainly for a student who wishes to visit India, the development of a basic iconographic vocabulary is essential, for deities such as the monkey Hanumān or the fierce Kālī confront one at every turn.

When the first European traders and travelers visited India, they were astonished at the multitude of images of the various deities which they saw there. They called them "idols" and described them with combined fascination and repugnance. For example, Ralph Fitch, who traveled as a merchant through north India in the 1500s writes of the images of deities in Banāras: "Their chiefe idols bee blacke and evill favoured, their mouths monstrous, their eares gilded and full of jewels, their teeth and eyes of gold, silver and glasse, some having one thing in their hands and some another."[27]

Fitch had no interpretive categories, save those of a very general Western Christian background, with which to make sense of what he saw. Three hundred years did little to aid interpretation. When M. A. Sherring lived in Banāras in the middle of the 1800s he could still write, after studying the city for a long time, of "the worship of uncouth idols, of monsters, of the liṅga and other indecent figures, and of a multitude of grotesque, ill-shapen, and hideous objects."[28] When Mark Twain traveled through India in the last decade of the nineteenth century, he brought a certain imaginative humor to the array of "idols" in Banāras, but he remained without what Arnheim would call "manageable models" for placing the visible data of India in a recognizable context. Of the "idols" he wrote, "And what a swarm of them there is! The town is a vast museum of idols — and all of them crude, misshapen, and ugly. They flock through one's dreams at night, a wild mob of nightmares."[29]

Without some interpretation, some visual hermeneutic, icons and images can be alienating rather than enlightening. Instead of being keys to understanding, they can kindle xenophobia and pose barriers to understanding by appearing as a "wild mob of nightmares," utterly foreign to and unassimilable by our minds. To understand India, we need to raise our eyes from the book to the image, but we also need some means of interpreting and comprehending the images we see.

The bafflement of many who first behold the array of Hindu images springs from the deep-rooted Western antagonism to imaging the divine at all. The Hebraic hostility to "graven images" expressed in the Commandments is echoed repeatedly in the Hebrew Bible: "You shall not make for yourself a graven image, or any likeness of anything that is in heaven above, or that is in the earth beneath, or that is in the water under the earth."

The Hebraic resistance to imaging the divine has combined with a certain distrust of the senses in the world of the Greek tradition as well. While the Greeks were famous for their anthropomorphic images of the gods, the prevalent suspicion in the philosophies of classical Greece was that "what the eyes reported was not true."[30] Like those of dim vision in Plato's cave, it was thought that people generally accept the mere shadows of reality as "true." Nevertheless,

Durgā as the Slayer of the Buffalo
Demon. India, Pallava, 8th century.
Height: 1.5 cm. Denman Waldo
Ross Collection, 27.171. Courtesy,
Museum of Fine Arts, Boston

Gaṇeśa, Guardian of the threshold, sitting above a doorway in Banāras

if dim vision described human perception of the ordinary world, the Greeks continued to use the notion of true vision to describe wisdom, that which is seen directly in the full light of day rather than obliquely in the shadowy light of the cave. Arnheim writes, "The Greeks learned to distrust the senses, but they never forgot that direct vision is the first and final source of wisdom. They refined the techniques of reasoning, but they also believed that, in the words of Aristotle, 'the soul never thinks without an image.'"[31]

On the whole, it would be fair to say that the Western traditions, especially the religious traditions of the "Book" — Judaism, Christianity, and Islam — have trusted the Word more than the Image as a mediator of the divine truth. The Qur'ān and the Hebrew Bible are filled with injunctions to "proclaim" and to "hear" the word. The ears were somehow more trustworthy than the eyes. In the Christian tradition this suspicion of the eyes and the image has been a particularly Protestant position.

And yet the visible image has not been without some force in the religious thinking of the West. The verbal icon of God as "Father" or "King" has had considerable power in shaping the Judeo-Christian religious imagination. The Orthodox Christian traditions, after much debate in the eighth and ninth centuries, granted an important place to the honoring of icons as those "windows" through one might look toward God. They were careful, however, to say that the icon should not be "realistic" and should be only two-dimensional. In the Catholic tradition as well, the art and iconography, especially of Mary and the saints, has had a long and rich history. And all three traditions of the "Book" have developed the art of embellishing the word into a virtual icon in the elaboration of calligraphic and decorative arts. Finally, it should be said that there is a great diversity within each of these traditions. The Mexican villager who comes on his knees to the Virgin of Guadalupe, leaves a bundle of beans, and lights a candle, would no doubt feel more at home in a Hindu temple than in a stark, white New England Protestant church. Similarly, the Moroccan Muslim woman who visits the shrines of Muslim saints, would find India less foreign than did the eleventh century Muslim scholar Alberuni, who wrote that "the Hindus entirely differ from us in every respect."[32]

Worshiping as God those "things" which are not God has been despised in the Western traditions as "idolatry," a mere bowing down to "sticks and stones." The difficulty with such a view of idolatry, however, is that anyone who bows down to such things clearly does not understand them to be sticks and stones. No people would identify themselves as "idolators," by faith. Thus, idolatry can be only an outsider's term for the symbols and visual images of some other culture. Theodore Roszak, writing in *Where the Wasteland Ends*, locates the "sin of idolatry" precisely where it belongs: in the eye of the beholder.[33]

In beginning to understand the consciousness of the Hindu worshiper who bows to "sticks and stones," an anecdote of the Indian novelist U. R. Anantha Murthy is provocative. He tells of an artist friend who was studying folk art in rural north India. Looking into one hut, he saw a stone daubed with red *kunkum* powder, and he asked the villager if he might bring the stone outside to photograph it. The villager agreed, and after the artist had photographed the stone he realized that he might have polluted this sacred object by moving it outside. Horrified, he apologized to the villager, who replied, "It doesn't matter. I will have to bring another stone and anoint *kunkum* on it." Anantha Murthy comments, "Any piece of stone on which he put *kunkum* became God for the peasant. What mattered was his faith, not the stone."[34] We might add that, of course, the stone matters too. If it did not, the peasant would not bother with a stone at all.

Unlike the zealous Protestant missionaries of a century ago, we are not much given to the use of the term "idolatry" to condemn what "other people" do. Yet those who misunderstood have still left us with the task of understanding, and they have raised an important and subtle issue in the comparative study of religion: What is the nature of the divine image? Is it considered to be intrinsically sacred? Is it a symbol of the sacred? A mediator of the sacred? How are images made, consecrated, and used, and what does this tell us about the way they are understood? But still another question remains to be addressed before we take up these topics. That is the question of the multitude of images. Why are there so many gods?

E. The Polytheistic Imagination

It is not only the image-making capacity of the Hindu imagination that confronts the Western student of Hinduism, but the bold Hindu polytheistic consciousness. Here too, in attempting to understand another culture, we discover one of the great myths of our own: the myth of monotheism. Myths are those "stories" we presuppose about the nature of the world and its structures of meaning. Usually we take our own myths so much for granted that it is striking to recognize them as "myths" which have shaped not only our religious viewpoint, but our ways of knowing. Even Westerners who consider themselves to be secular participate in the myth of monotheism: that in matters of ultimate importance, there is only One — one God, one Book, one Son, one Church, one Seal of the Prophets, one Nation under God. The psychologist James Hillman speaks of a "monotheism of consciousness" which has shaped our very habits of thinking, so that the autonomous, univocal, and independent personality is considered healthy; single-minded decision-making is considered a strength; and the concept of the independent ego as "number one" is considered normal.[35]

In entering into the Hindu world, one confronts a way of thinking which one might call "radically polytheistic," and if there is any "great divide" between the traditions of India and those of the West,

Gaṇeśa, Banāras folk art

it is in just this fact. Some may object that India has also affirmed Oneness as resolutely and profoundly as any culture on earth, and indeed it has. The point here, however, is that India's affirmation of Oneness is made in a context that affirms with equal vehemence the multitude of ways in which human beings have seen that Oneness and expressed their vision. Indian monotheism or monism cannot, therefore, be aptly compared with the monotheism of the West. The statement that "God is One" does not mean the same thing in India and the West.

At virtually every level of life and thought, India is polycentric and pluralistic. India, with what E. M. Forster called "her hundred mouths,"[36] has been the very exemplar of cultural multiplicity. There is geographical and racial diversity from the Pathans of the Punjab to the Dravidians of Tamilnād. There are fourteen major language groups. There is the elaborate social diversity of the caste system. There is the religious diversity of major religious traditions: the Hindus, Muslims, Sikhs, Christians, Buddhists, Jains, and Parsis. (As Mark Twain quipped in his diaries from India, "In religion, all other countries are paupers. India is the only millionaire."[37] And even within what is loosely called "Hinduism" there are many sectarian strands: Vaiṣṇavas, Śaivas, Śāktas, Smārtas, and others. Note that the very term *Hinduism* refers only to the "ism" of the land which early Muslims called "Hind," literally, the land beyond the Indus. Hinduism is no more, no less than the "ism" of India.

The diversity of India has been so great that it has sometimes been difficult for Westerners to recognize in India any underlying unity As the British civil servant John Strachey put it, speaking to an audience at Cambridge University in 1859, "There is no such country, and this is the first and most essential fact about India that can be learned. . . ."[38] Seeking recognizable signs of unity — common language, unifying religion, shared historical tradition — he did not see them in India.

In part, the unity of India, which Strachey and many others like him could not see, is in its cultural genius for embracing diversity, so that diversity unites, rather than divides. For example, there are the six philosophical traditions recognized as "orthodox." But they are not called "systems" in the sense in which we use that term. Rather, they are *darśanas*. Here the term means not the "seeing" of the deity, but the "seeing" of truth. There are many such *darśanas*, many "points of view" or "perspectives" on the truth. And although each has its own starting point, its own theory of causation, its own accepted enumeration of the means by which one can arrive at valid knowledge, these "ways of seeing" share a common goal — liberation — and they share the understanding that all their rivals are also "orthodox." Philosophical discourse, therefore, takes the form of an ongoing dialogue, in which the views of others are explained so that one can counter them with one's own view. Any "point of view" implicitly assumes that another point of view is possible.

Moving from the philosophical to the social sphere, there is the well-known diversity of interlocking and interdependent caste groups. On a smaller scale, there is the polycentric system of family authority, which is integral to the extended, joint family. Here not only the father and mother, but grandparents, aunts, and uncles serve as different loci of family authority and fulfill different needs.

Not unrelated to this complex polycentrism of the social structure is the polycentric imaging of the pantheon of gods and goddesses. Just as the social and institutional structures of the West have tended historically to mirror the patriarchal monotheism of the religious imagination, so have the social structure and family structure of India displayed the same tendency toward diversification that is visible in the complex polytheistic imagination. At times, the ordering of the diverse parts of the whole seems best described as hierarchical;[39] yet it is also true that the parts of the whole are knotted together in interrelations that seem more like a web than a ladder. The unity of India, both socially and religiously, is that of a complex whole. In a complex whole, the presupposition upon which oneness is based is not unity or sameness, but interrelatedness and diversity.

The German Indologist Betty Heimann uses the image of a crystal to describe this multiplex whole:

> Whatever Man sees, has seen or will see, is just one facet only of a crystal. Each of these facets from its due angle provides a correct viewpoint, but none of them alone gives a true all-comprehensive picture. Each serves in its proper place to grasp the Whole, and all of them combined come nearer to its full grasp. However, even the sum of them all does not exhaust all hidden possibilities of approach.[40]

The diversity of deities is part of the earliest Vedic history of the Hindu tradition. In the Ṛg Veda, the various gods are elaborately praised and in their individual hymns, each is praised as Supreme. Indra may in one hymn be called the "Sole Sovereign of Men and of Gods," and in the next hymn Varuṇa may be praised as the "Supreme Lord, Ruling the Spheres." Max Müller, who was the first great Western interpreter of the Vedas, searched for an adequate term to describe the religious spirit of this literature. It is not monotheism, although there certainly is a vision of divine supremacy as grand as the monotheistic vision. It is not really polytheism, at least if one understands this as the worship of many gods, each with partial authority and a limited sphere of influence. He saw that these Western terms did not quite fit the Hindu situation. To describe the deities of Hinduism, Müller coined the word *kathenotheism* — the worship of one god at a time. Each is exalted in turn. Each is praised as creator, source, and sustainer of the universe when one stands in the presence of that deity. There are many gods, but their multiplicity does not diminish the significance or power of any of them. Each of the great gods may serve as a lens through which the whole of reality is clearly seen.

The spirit which Müller saw in the Vedic hymns continues to be of great significance in many aspects of Indian religious life. To celebrate one deity, one sacred place, one temple, does not mean there is no room for the celebration of another. Each has its hour. One learns, for example, that there are three gods in the tradition today: Viṣṇu, Śiva, and the Devī. But it is clear from their hymns and rites that these deities are not regarded as having partial powers. Each is seen, by those who are devotees, as Supreme in every sense. Each is alone seen to be the creator, sustainer, and final resting place of all. Each has assembled the minor deities and autochthonous divinities of India into its own entourage. The frustration of students encountering the Hindu array of deities for the first time is, in part, the frustration of trying to get it all straight and to place the various deities and their spouses, children, and manifestations in a fixed pattern in relation to one another. But the pattern of these imaged deities is like the pattern of the kaleidoscope: one twist of the wrist and the relational pattern of the pieces changes.

In the Bṛhadāraṇyaka Upaniṣad, a seeker named Vidagdha Śākalya approaches the sage Yājñavalkya with the question, "How many gods are there, Yājñavalkya?"[41]

"Three thousand three hundred and six," he replied.
"Yes," said he, "but just how many gods are there, Yājñavalkya?"
"Thirty-three."
"Yes," said he, "but just how many gods are there, Yājñavalkya?"
"Six."
"Yes," said he, "but just how many gods are there, Yājñavalkya?"
"Three."
"Yes," said he, "but just how many gods are there, Yājñavalkya?"
"Two."
"Yes," said he, "but just how many gods are there, Yājñavalkya?"
"One and a half."
"Yes," said he, "but just how many gods are there, Yājñavalkya?"
"One."

Yājñavalkya continues by explaining the esoteric knowledge of the different enumerations of the gods. But the point he makes is hardly esoteric. It is not the secret knowledge of the forest sages, but is part of the shared presuppositions of the culture. In any Hindu temple there will be, in addition to the central sanctum, a dozen surrounding shrines to other deities: Ganeśa, Hanumān, Durgā, Gaurī, and so on. Were one to ask any worshiper Vidagdha Śākalya's question, "How many gods are there?" one would hear Yājñavalkya's response from even the most uneducated. "Sister, there are many gods. There is Śiva here, and there is Viṣṇu, Gaṇeśa, Hanumān, Gaṅgā, Durgā, and the others. But of course, there is really only one. These many are differences of name and form."

"Name and form" — *nāma rūpa* — is a common phrase, used often to describe the visible, changing world of *saṁsāra* and the multiple world of the gods. There is one reality, but the names and forms by which it is known are different. It is like clay, which is one, but which takes on various names and forms as one sees it in bricks, earthen vessels, pots, and dishes. While some philosophers would contend that the perception of the one is a higher and clearer vision of the truth than the perception of the many, Hindu thought is most distinctive for its refusal to make the one and the many into opposites. For most, the manyness of the divine is not superseded by oneness. Rather, the two are held simultaneously and are inextricably related. As one of the great praises of the Devī puts it: "Nameless and Formless Thou art, O Thou Unknowable. All forms of the universe are Thine: thus Thou art known."[42]

The very images of the gods portray in visual form the multiplicity and the oneness of the divine, and they display the tensions and the seeming contradictions that are resolved in a single mythic image. Many of the deities are made with multiple arms, each hand bearing an emblem or a weapon, or posed in a gesture, called a *mudrā*. The emblems and *mudrās* indicate the various powers that belong to the deity. Gaṇeśa's lotus is an auspicious sign, while his hatchet assures that in his role as guardian of the threshold he is armed to prevent the passage of miscreants. The Devī Durgā has eight arms and in her many hands she holds the weapons and emblems of all the gods, who turned their weapons over to her to kill the demon of chaos. Multiple faces and eyes are common. The creator Brahmā, for example, has four faces, looking in each of the four directions. Śiva and Viṣṇu are depicted together in one body, each half with the emblems appropriate to its respective deity. Similarly, Śiva is sometimes depicted in the Ardhanārīśvara, "Half-Woman God" form, which is half Śiva and half Śakti. The androgynous image is split down the middle: one-breasted, clothed half in male garments and half in female. In a similar way, Rādhā and Kṛṣṇa are sometimes shown as entwined together in such a fashion that, while one could delineate two separate figures, they appear to the eye as inseparably one.

The variety of names and forms in which the divine has been perceived and worshiped in the Hindu tradition is virtually limitless. If one takes some of the persistent themes of Hindu creation myths as a starting point, the world is not only the embodiment of the divine, but the very body of the divine. The primal person, Puruṣa, was divided up in the original sacrifice to become the various parts of the cosmos (Ṛg Veda X.90). Or, in another instance, the original germ or egg from which the whole of creation evolved was a unitary whole, containing in a condensed form

Rādhā and Kṛṣṇa, Folk art from Orissa

Viṣṇu, 15th Century bronze Tanjore Art Gallery, No. 50

within it the whole of the potential and life of the universe (Ṛg Veda X.121; Chāndogya Upaniṣad 3.19; Aitareya Upaniṣad 1.1). If all names and forms evolved from the original seed of the universe, then all have the potential for revealing the nature of the whole. While far-sighted visionaries may describe the one Brahman by the negative statement, "Not this . . . Not this . . . ," still from the standpoint of this world, one can as well describe Brahman with the infinite affirmation, "It is this . . . It is this. . . ." The two approaches are inseparable. As Betty Heimann put it, ". . . whenever the uninitiated outsider is surprised, embarrassed, or repulsed by the exuberant paraphernalia of materialistic display in Hindu cult, he must keep in mind that, side by side with these, stands the utmost abstraction in religious feeling and thought, the search for the *Neti-Neti* Brahman, the 'not this, not that,' which denies itself to all representations, higher or lower."[43]

CHAPTER 2

The Nature of the Hindu Image

A. The Aniconic and the Iconic Image

THE IMAGE which Hindus come to "see" in a temple or an open-air shrine may be anthropomorphic in appearance, albeit with fantastic features which may little resemble any *anthropos* of flesh and blood, or it may be theriomorphic, like Hanumān with the body of a monkey or Gaṇeśa with the head of an elephant. On the other hand, it may have no discernible "form" at all; it may be a rock outcropping or a smooth stone. In exploring the nature of images in the Hindu context we must make a further distinction between the iconic and the aniconic image. For our purposes, the iconic image is one which is representational; it has a recognizable "likeness" to its mythic subject. The Latin *icon* or the Greek *eikon* means "likeness" or "image" and calls to mind the icons of Orthodox Christianity which show a likeness of Christ or Mary. By contrast, the aniconic images are those symbolic forms which, although they refer to a deity, do not attempt any anthropomorphic form or any representational likeness. The plain cross, for example, is aniconic, as is the *liṅga* of Śiva or the natural stone *śālagrāma* of Viṣṇu.

India has ancient traditions of both iconic and aniconic image-making. The terracotta female "deities" of the Indus Valley, for example, are certainly full-bodied representations of the female form, although it is not clear how they were utilized ritually. On the other hand, the Vedic ritual tradition of the Aryan newcomers has generally been seen as aniconic, for there is no evidence of images or of permanent temples or sanctuaries. Vedic religion consisted primarily of domestic and kingly sacrificial rites centered around the sacred fire. The fire was both a focus and a vehicle of ritual activity. The construction of the Vedic fire altar was the symbolic

Stones daubed with vermilion at the base of a tree

construction of the "image" of the primordial creator, Prajāpati, and therefore was also the symbolic construction of the world, which emerged from Prajāpati. The fire has continued to be utilized as an aniconic image of the divine, and it has a central place in many Hindu rites. Although in the Vedic period there is virtually no evidence to indicate the use of iconic images in worship,[44] it is important to note that the Vedic poets were image-makers in another sense: they created vivid images of the gods in their poetry. There was the Sun, the witness of the world with heavenly eye; Agni, with seven red tongues, seven faces, and gleaming hair; and Indra, the warrior, who carried the thunderbolt.

The Aniconic Image.

While the fire might be considered an ancient aniconic "image," I want to turn here to the traditions of aniconic imaging that have emerged from the folk traditions of India and continue to have influence all over India today. The most ancient non-Vedic cultus of India was almost certainly aniconic. Stones, natural symbols, and earthen mounds signified the presence of a deity long before the iconic images of the great gods came to occupy the *sancta* of temples and shrines. Much of India, especially rural India, still designates its local deities in this way, be they *devīs, bhairavas, yakṣas,* or others. The villager whom the urban artist "discovered" sanctifying a stone with red *kunkum* powder is at home in this tradition.

Many of the deities of this ancient cultus were and are local deities, such as the *grāma devatās,* "village deities," or task-specific deities, such as Śītalā who has to do with fever-diseases or the *mātṛkās* ("mothers"), who have to do with birth and childhood. Within their areas of jurisdiction they both cause and cure disease, bring both safety and harm. There are also deities of what Coomaraswamy has called the "life-cult," namely the *yakṣas* and *nāgas,* associated respectively with trees and pools.[45] They too are propitiated as both beneficent and potentially fierce. In their beneficent form they are associated with well-being, and the plump, hospitable Gaṇeśa is one heir of this ancient family of deities.

The form of worship offered to these deities included sprinkling the stone with water, making offerings of flowers, food, cloth and incense, and smearing the stone with various substances. These are essentially the types of rites which became the constituent elements of Hindu *pūjā* in the later tradition. Frequently, however, the ancient rites also included meat and liquor as part of the food offering, and blood as part of the smearing or anointing of the stone. This type of worship, called *bali,* is still offered to certain autochthonous deities. Those who accept sacrificial offerings may sometimes be offered blood, but more frequently the anointing today is with vermilion paint or dry red *kunkum* powder.

In addition to the many local deities whose presence is marked by vermilion smeared stones, there are a number of aniconic images which have attained a prominent place in wider pan-Indian ritual. The *śālagrāma* stone, for instance, is called a *svarūpa,* a "natural form" of Viṣṇu. This smooth stone, found primarily in the bed of the Gaṇḍakī River in Nepal, is inherently sacred, so it needs no consecration rites when it is installed for worship in a temple or home shrine. For the Hindu, it *is* Viṣṇu. Similarly, the stones of Mount Govardhan in Vraj, the north Indian homeland of Kṛṣṇa, are known as *svarūpa* forms of Kṛṣṇa, and they are taken from Govardhan to be worshiped in homes and temples all over Vraj and, indeed, all over India.[46]

In the sacred River Narmadā, which runs to the west across

central India, there is another special stone — the *bāṇa liṅga* which is said to be a natural form of Śiva. This smooth, cylindrical stone may be worshiped as Śiva without any rite of consecration. The *bāṇa liṅga* is considered a *svayambhū*, "self-born," *liṅga*.

Śiva liṅga near the riverfront, Kedār ghāṭ, Banāras

The *liṅga* is perhaps the best known of India's aniconic images. Not all *liṅgas*, of course, are *bāṇa liṅgas*. Most are fashioned by artisans and established in Śiva temples by rites of consecration. It is primarily in this form that Śiva is worshiped in the temples of India.

The *liṅga* is often referred to as a "phallic" symbol, and for those European travelers and missionaries who saw it as an unmistakeable "likeness" of the phallus, rather than an aniconic image of Śiva, the *liṅga* evoked the strongest feelings of moral outrage. For example, the Abbé Dubois, an eighteenth century French missionary, described it as "obscene," and wrote, "It is incredible, it is impossible to believe, that in inventing this vile superstition the religious teachers of India intended that the people should render direct worship to objects the very names of which, among civilized nations, are an insult to decency."[47] It is true that some of the myths of the *liṅga's* origin are myths of castration, and it is true that the earliest *liṅga* image (the Guḍimallam *liṅga*, ca. 100 B.C.E.) is clearly phallic in form.[48] However, the *liṅga* as it is worshiped in India today is more accurately seen as an aniconic image, and the myths of the Śaivas for whom this symbol is significant, see its origins in a magnificent hierophany of a fiery column of light, rather than in a primal act of castration.[49] Those who worship Śiva in the *liṅga* form are consistently appalled to hear it understood as phallic, and again we suspect the interpretations of the "eye of the beholder."

The *liṅga* consists of two parts: the vertical stone shaft, which may be seen as the male component, Śiva, and the circular horizontal base, called a *yonī* or *pīṭha*, which is the female component, Śakti. The wedge-shaped spout is also part of the *yoni* and serves as a drain to carry away the water offerings poured upon the *liṅga*. Together the *liṅga* and *pīṭha* form the Śiva-Śakti symbol of divine unity. The one who is commonly called "Śiva" is seen in the *liṅga* as both Śiva and Śakti, male and female, divine spirit and divine matter, transcendent and immanent, aloof and active. In addition, the shaft of the *liṅga* is often said to have three sections, representing Brahmā, Viṣṇu, and Śiva respectively. The word *liṅga* means "mark" or "sign" as well as "phallus," and it is in the former sense, as the sign of Śiva, Mahādeva, the "Great Lord," that the *liṅga* is honored in the *sancta* of the many temples and shrines of India.

There are many other types of aniconic images which present the Hindu worshiper with the deity's token or sign, rather than the deity's face. Of course, the various gods have many emblems by which they can be recognized, including weapons, such as Rāma's bow, and animal mounts, such as Durgā's lion. Here, however, we are concerned with those emblems that are honored as the very embodiment of the god. Among these there is the full pot of water, indicating the presence of the *devī*;[50] the lotiform sun disc, marking the place of the Sun, Sūrya; the footprints, (*pādukās*) showing the presence of Viṣṇu or a saint or, in former days, the Buddha; and the *yantra*, the geometric interlocking triangles signifying the *devī*. Finally, among aniconic images are those embodiments of divinity which are aspects of nature, such as the River Gaṅgā or the River Yamunā; the *tulsī* (basil) plant; the *aśvattha* (fig) tree; and the Sun.

Four-Faced Liṅga. Fifth century, from Nachna-Kutara in Madhya Pradesh. Photography courtesy of American Institute of Indian Studies, Rāmnagar, Banāras

The Iconic Image

Just as the term icon conveys the sense of a "likeness," so do the Sanskrit words *pratikṛti* and *pratimā* suggest the "likeness" of the image to the deity it presents. The common word for such images, however, is *mūrti*, which is defined in Sanskrit as "anything which has definite shape and limits," "a form, body, figure," "an embodiment, incarnation, manifestation,"[51] Thus the *mūrti* is more than a likeness; it is the deity itself taken "form."

The uses of the word *mūrti* in the Upaniṣads and the Bhagavad Gītā suggest that the form *is* its essence. The flame is the *mūrti* of fire (Śvetāśvatara Upaniṣad 1.13), or the year is the *mūrti* of time (Maitri Upaniṣad 6.14). When the formless waters of creation were brooded upon by the creator, form (*mūrti*) emerged (Aitareya Upaniṣad 3.2). It is form (*mūrti*) which takes shape in the womb of the unfathomable Brahman who gives birth to all forms (Bhagavad Gītā 14.3-4). While the word *mūrti* does not commonly mean the icon of a deity in this early period, it is significant that the term itself suggests the congealing of form and limit from that larger reality which has no form or limit. However, the *mūrti* is a body-taking, a manifestation, and is not different from the reality itself.

Another common word for the iconic image is *vigraha*, a word which means "body." As a noun, *vigraha* comes from a verbal root (*vi* + *gṛh*) which means "to grasp, to catch hold of." The *vigraha* is that form which enables the mind to grasp the nature of God.

The images of the gods are not "likenesses" of any earthly form. They are fantastic forms, with multiple heads and arms, with blue, green, or vermilion coloring, or with part-animal bodies. They are not intended to "represent" earthly realities, but rather to present divine realities. They stretch the human imagination toward the divine by juxtaposing earthly realities in an unearthly way. To the extent that the *vigraha* is a "body," it is anthropomorphic. But the body with Śiva's three eyes, or Viṣṇu's four arms, or Skanda's six heads is hardly like our own. The things of the world we can see well enough all about us, but for the Indian religious artist the task of image-making was giving shape to those things we cannot readily see.

The iconic image has had a central role in Hindu worship for about two thousand years. Leaving aside the images of the Indus Valley, the first anthropomorphic images were those of the stout *yakṣas* and voluptuous *yakṣis*, whose worship constituted the prevailing popular cultus of India.[52] It is not surprising that the images of such "life-cult" deities — who were and who remain most intimately involved in the vital concerns of birth and growth, sickness and death — should be among the first fashioned in stone by craftsmen, beginning in the Mauryan period in the third century B.C.E.[53]

In the first century C.E., the Buddha — previously represented by aniconic symbols such as his footprints — came to be depicted in an anthropomorphic image. This happened both in the Hellenistic school of art which developed in northwest India at the Asian crossroads called Gandhāra and in the religious center of Mathurā in central north India. In Gandhāra, the Buddha's form was Greco-Roman in style. In Mathurā, however, the early Buddhas seem to inherit their style and bearing from the sturdy *yakṣas* of the Mauryan age.

While there are a few early images of Hindu gods, such as the second century B.C.E. reliefs of Indra and Sūrya at Bhājā on the western *ghāts* south of Bombay, they were not established as cult icons. Rather, the Bhājā reliefs were part of a Buddhist monastic retreat. The real flowering of the Hindu divine image took place in the Gupta period (4th-7th centuries), called the Golden Age of Indian Art. During this time some of the earliest Hindu stone temples were constructed: the Durgā temple at Aihole near Bādāmi and the Viṣṇu temple at Deogarh, with its famous image of Viṣṇu reclining on the serpent Śeṣa.[54]

The development of images used in worship occurred at the same time as the development of the temples which houses the images. After the Gupta period, the impetus for such artistic and religious creativity came primarily from the regional dynasties of India. In Orissa in the east, there was an era of temple construction in Bhuvaneśvar (8th-11th centuries); nearby at Koṇārak the famous temple of the Sun was built (13th century). The temples of Khajurāho were patronized by the Candella kings of central India (11th century). In the west, the rock-cut temple at Ellūrā was created during the Rāṣṭrakūta dynasty (8th-9th centuries). In the south, the seaside temples of Mahābalipuram were built under the patronage of the Pallavas (7th-9th centuries); Tanjore was built by the Coḷas (11th century); Vijayanagar was built by refugees from the north during the Muslim invasions (16th century); and Madurai

Śiva Naṭarāja. Courtesy of the Dora Porter Mason Collection, Denver Art Museum, Denver, Colorado

was built by the Nayak dynasty (17th century). All these sanctuaries provided the stimulus for a wide variety of sculptural works, not only the prolific imagery of the temple exteriors, but the icons which occupied the inner *sancta* and the side shrines as well.[55]

The traditions of sculptural representation of the gods, as they emerged during these centuries, served both theological and narrative functions. First, Hindu images were visual "theologies," and they continue to be "read" as such by Hindus today. For example, the icon of the four-armed Śiva dancing in a ring of fire reveals the many aspects of this god in one visual symbol.[56] The flaming circle in which he dances is the circle of creation and destruction called *saṁsāra* (the earthly round of birth and death) or *māyā* (the illusory world). The Lord who dances in the circle of this changing world holds in two of his hands the drum of creation and the fire of destruction. He displays his strength by crushing the bewildered demon underfoot. Simultaneously, he shows his mercy by raising his palm to the worshiper in the "fear-not" gesture and, with another hand, by pointing to his upraised foot, where the worshiper may take refuge. It is a wild dance, for the coils of his ascetic's hair are flying in both directions, and yet the facial countenance of the Lord is utterly peaceful and his limbs in complete balance. Around one arm twines the *nāga*, the ancient serpent which he has incorporated into his sphere of power and wears now as an ornament. In his hair sits the mermaid River Gaṅgā, who landed first on Śiva's hair when she fell from heaven to earth. Such an image as the dancing Śiva engages the eye and extends one's vision of the nature of this god, using simple, subtle, and commonly understood gestures and emblems. In any image, it is the combination and juxtaposition of these gestures and emblems which expresses the ambiguities, the tensions, and the paradoxes which Hindus have seen in the deity: Śiva holds *both* the drum and the flame; the Goddess Kālī simultaneously wears a gory garland of skulls and gestures her protection; Viṣṇu appears with Śiva's emblems in his own hands. This image-world of India is what Betty Heimann has aptly called "visible thought."[57]

Images are not only visual theologies, they are also visual scriptures. The many myths of the tradition are narrated in living stone. In the West, the great carved portals of the Chartres Cathedral, for example, presented the stories, the ethics, and the eschatology of

"The Descent of the Gaṅgā" from Ravalphadi cave, Aihole (Bijapur, Mysore). Late 6th century sandstone. Photography courtesy of the American Institute of Indian Studies, Rāmnagar, Banāras

the Christian tradition for the vast majority who could not read. Even earlier, Pope Gregory I had recognized the didactic value of images: "For that which a written document is to those who can read, that a picture is to the unlettered who look at it. Even the unlearned see in that what course they ought to follow; even those who do not know the alphabet can read there."[58] In India, some of the earliest sculptural reliefs, on the railing around the Buddhist *stūpa* at Bhārhut, were medallions which told the popular Buddhist Jātaka tales. Similarly, the great temples of Hindu India often displayed bas relief portrayals of myths and legends. In the late Gupta image depicted here, the story of the descent of the River Gaṅgā is told: Śiva stands, flanked by his wife Pārvatī and the ascetic Bhagīratha, who performed austerities for thousands of years in order to bring the Gaṅgā to earth. Bhagīratha, all skin and bones, is shown in an ascetic posture, holding his arms up in the air, while the Triple-Pathed Gaṅgā — flowing in heaven, on the earth, and in the netherworlds — hovers over Śiva's head in the form of three mermaids.

In India today, this narrative and didactic tradition is carried on in folk art. One will see the episodes of myth painted on the walls of public buildings, private homes, and temples. Hanumān carries the mountain full of healing herbs to revive the armies of Rāma in Laṅka, or Viṣṇu emerges from a turtle in one of his many world-rescuing *avatāras*. Local and regional legends are elaborated as well, such as those of the Goddess Mīnākṣī and Śiva Sundareśvara painted in the temple compound at Madurai.

Modern technology has been eagerly employed for the presentation of traditional myths. In Indian commercial films, for example, one will see Śiva, standing in his animal hides in the high Himālayas, with animated artificial snakes swaying to and fro about his neck,[59] or one may see a cartoon rendering of the primordial contest of the gods and the demons when they churned the Sea of Milk.[60] In several of India's newest temple complexes, such as the Tulsī Mānas temple in Vārāṇasī, there are Disneyland-type plastic figures of the gods, with moving parts and voices. For example, at the door of Tulsī Mānas temple stands Hanumān, the monkey servant of Lord Rāma, tearing open his chest every few seconds to reveal the Lord within his heart and uttering the words "Rām Rām!" Such images attract villagers from many miles away. These people watch the animated scenes with fascination and devotion, and they linger to tell one another the stories and to remind one another of the details. Finally, the mass printing of color reproductions has extended the availability of images. Hindus are great consumers of these polychrome glossy images of the gods and their deeds. Taking them home from a temple or a place of pilgrimage, the devout may place such images in the home shrine. Thus one may have *darśan* not only of the image, but, of the picture of the image as well!

Hanumān and Viṣṇu's Tortoise-Avatāra, from the exterior wall of the Ratneśvara temple, Banāras

B. The Ritual Uses of the Image

How is the divine image regarded by Hindus? And how is it used in a ritual context? Pursuing these questions is important to our understanding of the nature of the divine image which Hindus "see."

Two principal attitudes may be discerned in the treatment of images. The first is that the image is primarily a focus for concentration, and the second is that the image is the embodiment of the divine.

In the first view, the image is a kind of *yantra*, literally a "device" for harnessing the eye and the mind so that the one-pointedness of thought (*ekāgrata*) which is fundamental to meditation can be attained. The image is a support for meditation. As the *Viṣṇu Sāṁhitā*, a ritual *āgama* text, puts it:

> Without a form, how can God be mediated upon? If (He is) without any form, where will the mind fix itself? When there is nothing for the mind to attach itself to, it will slip away from meditation or will glide into a state of slumber. Therefore the wise will meditate on some form, remembering, however, that the form is a superimposition and not a reality.[61]

The Jābāla Upaniṣad goes even a step further, intimating that such an image, while it may be a support for the beginner, is of absolutely no use to the yogi. "Yogins see Śiva in the soul and not in images. Images are meant for the imagination of the ignorant."[62]

It is the second attitude toward images that most concerns us in the context of this essay. That is, that the image is the real embodiment of the deity. It is not just a device for the focusing of human vision, but is charged with the presence of the god. This stance toward images emerged primarily from the devotional *bhakti* movement, which cherished the personal Lord "with qualities" (*saguṇa*) and which saw the image as one of the many ways in which the Lord becomes accessible to men and women, evoking their affections.

In the early theistic traditions of the Bhāgavatas or Pāñcarātras, who emphasized devotional worship (*pūjā*) rather than the Vedic sacrifice (*yajña*), the image was considered to be one of the five forms of the Lord. The five are the Supreme form (*para*), the emanations or powers of the Supreme (*vyūha*), the immanence of the Supreme in the heart of the individual and in the heart of the universe (*antaryāmin*), the incarnations of the Supreme (*vibhava*), and, finally, the presence of the Supreme Lord in a properly consecrated image (*arcā*).[63] Later, the Śrī Vaiṣṇavas used the term *arcāvatāra* to refer to the "image-incarnation" of the Lord: the form Viṣṇu graciously takes so that he may be worshiped by his devotees.[64]

Indeed, the very theology of the Śrī Vaiṣṇava community, as articulated by Rāmānuja in the 11th century, is based on the faith that the Lord is characterized both by his utter Supremacy (*paratva*) and his gracious Accessibility (*saulabhya*).[65]

God has become accessible not only in incarnations, but also in images. In the *Bhagavad Gītā* (4.11), Kṛṣṇa tells Arjuna, "In whatever way people approach me, in that way do I show them favor." The word *bhajāmi* translated here as "I show favor," is from the same root as *bhakti*. It could equally be translated "in that way do I love them," or "in that way do I share myself with them." Rāmānuja, in commenting on this passage, says that it means "in that way do I make myself visible (*darśayāmi*) to them."[66] He goes on to comment, "God does not only rescue those, who resort to him in the shape of one of his *avatāras*, by descending into that shape alone, but He reveals himself to all who resort to him, whatever the shape in which they represent him."[67]

Following Rāmānuja, another theologian of the Śrī Vaiṣṇava movement, Piḷḷai Lokācārya, writes of the grace by which the Lord enters and dwells in the image for the sake of the devotee:

> This is the greatest grace of the Lord, that being free He becomes bound, being independent He becomes dependent for all His service on His devotee. . . . In other forms the man belonged to God but behold the supreme sacrifice of Īśvara, here the Almighty becomes the property of the devotee. . . . He carries Him about, fans Him, feeds Him, plays with Him — yea, the Infinite has become finite, that the child soul may grasp, understand and love Him."[68]

The image, which may be seen, bathed, adorned, touched, and honored does not stand *between* the worshiper and the Lord, somehow receiving the honor properly due to the Supreme Lord. Rather, because the image is a form of the Supreme Lord, it is precisely the image that facilitates and enhances the close relationship of the worshiper and God and makes possible the deepest outpouring of emotions in worship.

In observing Hindu worship, in the home or in the temple, many Western students are baffled by the sense in which it appears to be an elaborate form of "playing house" with God. The image is wakened in the morning, honored with incense and song, dressed, and fed. Throughout the day, other such rites appropriate to the time of day are performed until, finally, the deity is put to bed in the evening.

How is one to honor God? What human acts and gestures most directly convey the devotion of *bhakti*? For Hindus and for people of many religious traditions, they are the gestures of humility, with which a servant approaches his master, or a host his guest — gestures such as bowing, kneeling, prostrating, and, in the Hindu world, touching the feet of a revered superior. In addition to such servant-master gestures, however, the Hindus utilize the entire range of intimate and ordinary domestic acts as an important part of ritual. These are common, affectionate activities, family activities, which are symbolically powerful because of their very simplicity and their domestic nature: cooking, eating, serving, washing, dressing, waking, and putting to sleep. These are precisely the acts which ordinary people have most carefully refined through daily practice with loved ones in the home. In summary, Hindu worship reveals not only an attitude of honor but also an attitude of affection in the range of ritual act and gesture utilized in the treatment of the image.

The general term for rites of worship and honor is *pūjā*. The simple lay rites of making offerings of flowers and water, and receiving both *darśan*, the "sight of the deity, and *prasād*, the sanctified food offerings, may be called *pūjā*. More specifically, however, *pūjā* consists of elaborate forms of worship performed in the home by the householder and in the temple by special priests called *pūjārīs* who are designated for that purpose. These rites involve the presentation of a number of articles of worship, called *upacāras*, "honor offerings," to the deity. The number of *upacāras* presented may vary, but sixteen is considered a proper number for a complete *pūjā*. The *upacāras* include food, water, fresh leaves, sandalwood perfume, incense, betel nuts, and cloth. They are the type of hospitality offerings with which one would honor a guest, or a revered elder, or a king. In addition to such tangible offerings, the waving of the fan and the flywhisk are considered *upacāras*, since they are pleasing to the deity, and the rite of circumambulation is an *upacāra*, since it shows honor to the deity.

An important *upacāra* is the honoring of the deity with light. The priest or the householder slowly circles a five-wicked oil lamp or camphor lamp before the deity, often to the accompaniment of the ringing of handbells and the singing of hymns. This lamp-offering is called *āratī*, and the rite is so central to Hindu worship that *āratī* has become the common general name for the daily rites of honoring the deity, often replacing the term *pūjā* completely. In a temple there will ordinarily be several *āratīs* during the day and into the evening.

What notion of the image is revealed in the presentation of these *upacāras*? Does the deity really enjoy the smell of incense and the cooling refreshment of water? Is the deity really bothered by the heat and irritated by flies? Does the deity really wake up each morning and go to bed each night?

First, it must be said that most Hindus, especially of devotional sectarian movements like the Śrī Vaiṣṇavas, take the notion of image-incarnation quite seriously. The image is a divine "descent" of the Supreme Lord who entrusts himself to human caretaking. In the image-incarnation, one sees evidence of the theological notion expressed by Piḷḷai Lokācārya that people not only depend upon God, but God is willingly dependent upon people, upon their nurturance and caretaking. The worship of the child Kṛṣṇa, who elicits the most spontaneous and tender of human parental emotions, is another instance of the divine-human mutuality which is the essence of *bhakti*. *Bhakti* comes from a Sanskrit verb which means "to share," and *bhakti* is relational love, shared by both God and the devotee. There is no docetic notion of incarnation here. Remember that the docetic view was a "heresy" in the early Christian tradition, because it alleged that Jesus, although he appeared to be a man, did not really experience the thirst, the delight, and the pain of the human condition. While Hindus would not call such a view "heresy," they would certainly find it inhospitable not to offer the Lord water on the presumption that he does not experience thirst! In short, the image-incarnation *is* the divine guest, and it must be treated as such.

A further point might be made about these honor-offerings, namely that all ritual offerings and acts constitute a human grammar of devotion and really have nothing to do with the image at all. In other words, we show honor with these fruits and flowers because they are the most beautiful offerings that all people, even the poor, can afford. And we show honor with these particular gestures of reverence and nurture because these are the gestures of honor and devotion we know best. Whisking away the flies and offering a drink of water is *our language*, and not God's necessity.

Finally, what of the sense appeal of these honor offerings? The incense, the flowers, the lights, the chanting and hymnody, the food offerings — all this delights the senses, and not only the senses of the deity, but the senses of the worshiper as well. As Rāmānuja writes in his Bhagavad Gītā commentary (4.11), enlarging upon the words of Kṛṣṇa: "I suit myself in a manner that I am to them not only a visible demonstration, but they may enjoy me by every one of their sense faculties and in all diverse ways."[69] Hindu worship, therefore is certainly not an occasion for yogic withdrawing of the senses "as a tortoise withdraws its limbs,"[70] but it is rather an occasion for awakening the senses and directing them toward the divine. Entering the temple, a worshiper clangs a big overhead bell. The energy of the senses is harnessed to the apprehension of God. Thus, it is not only vision that is refined by *darśan*, but the other senses as well are focused, ever more sharply, on God.

Another way in which Hindu ritual provides some insight into the meaning of the image is in the simultaneous worship of multiple images. While the Śrī Vaiṣṇava temple will contain the image of Viṣṇu, flanked perhaps by his consorts Śrī and Bhū, there are many temples and homes in which there is no such single focus of devotion. The broad sectarian group called the Smārtas, for example, practice a form of worship called *pañcāyatana pūjā*, the "five-altar *pūjā*," in which five deities — usually Viṣṇu, Śiva, Sūrya, Devī and Gaṇeśa — are honored in a single geometrical diagram, with four images situated in the four directions and one in the center. Any one of these deities may occupy the center of this *maṇḍala* of deities. The very fact of the five reminds one that the presence of the God worshiped here transcends any one single form.[71]

The rites of *āvāhana* ("bidding") and *visarjana* ("dismissal") which very often open and close the period of worship also illumine something of the meaning of the image. *Āvāhana* is the "calling," the "bidding" of the deity at the commencement of worship. For example, Śiva may be invoked to be present in the *liṅga* with these words "O Lord, who protects the world, graciously be present in this *liṅga* until the end of the worship."[72] Similarly, when the *pūjā* is over, the deity is given leave to depart, with a prayer of dismissal: "O excellent gods, O Supreme Śiva, return now to your own abode so that you may come again for the benefit of the worshiper."[73]

Kṛṣṇa as Dvārākanāth Dvārakā, Gujarāt

While it is believed that God is present continually in any consecrated image of *liṅga*, the bidding and dismissal prayers provide a special framing of the ritual honor-offerings, and they make it clear that the omnipresent God is in no sense restricted by the multiple "image-incarnations" it undertakes.

There are some images, however, which are not permanently consecrated, and for these the bidding and dismissal constitute the temporal boundaries of the life of the image. For instance, the Goddess is asked to take up residence in the images especially made for each year's Durgā Pūjā, and at the end of the festival she is invited to depart, whereupon the images are disposed of. Even more dramatic is the "momentary" *kṣanika liṅga*, a lump of clay fashioned by the worshiper, perhaps in the palm of her hand. Śiva is asked to be present, the worshiper offers her prayers along with perhaps a flower and some water, and then Śiva is given leave to go. Again the lump of clay is but clay, and the worshiper throws it away, taking care to place it in a river or temple tank.[74]

All these ritual acts are premised on a common view of the nature of the image: that God is present in the image, whether for a moment, for a week, or forever. It is this fact of presence which is at the basis of *darśan*. People come to see because there is something very powerful there to see.

C. The Creation and Consecration of Images

How are divine images made? And in what way do they become invested with the presence that makes them not simply statues, but the abodes of deities?

There are many Sanskrit texts, based on ancient traditions transmitted orally, which deal with iconography and iconometry. They are the texts of artists, called *śilpins*, who make images. These *śilpaśāstras* treat image-making, along with architecture and the building of cities.[75] For each particular deity, these works specify the proper proportion of the parts of the body, the appropriate postures, the appropriate number of arms, the gestures of the hands (*mudrās*), the emblems and weapons to be held in the hands, and the appropriate animal mount (*vāhana*). Thus, the fashioning of the image is not left to the "imagination" of the individual artist.

A single god does not have a single form, of course, but may appear in a variety of traditional poses which reveal aspects of that god's nature or episodes in the god's mythology. Śiva, for example, may be depicted in the aniconic *liṅga* form, as a dancer (Naṭarāja), as a meditating ascetic (Dakṣiṇāmūrti), as the husband of Pārvatī (Kalyāṇasundara), as the destroyer of demons (Tripurāntaka, for example), as the half-woman god (Ardhanārīśvara), or as the one who emerges bodily out of the *liṅga* (Liṅgodbhava).[76] The *śāstras* enumerate the various poses and specify the details for each.

An image is also supposed to be beautiful, since it will be the abode of a deity. As the scholar J. N. Banerjea states in his extensive work on iconography, "A well executed image, if it follows the rules of proportion laid down in the *śilpaśāstras* and is pleasing to the eye, invites the deity to reside in it and is particularly auspicious to the worshippers."[77] What is beautiful, however, is also defined by the *śāstras*: "Only an image made in accordance with the canon can be called beautiful; some may think that beautiful which corresponds to their own fancy, but that not in accordance with the canon is unlovely to the discerning eye."[78] The *śāstras* assure that the image is not simply the expression of an individual artist, but the "written image" — the icon — of the divine.

From beginning to end the fashioning of an image is governed by ritual prescriptions. If the image is to be made of wood, for example, the image-maker is told which particular kinds of trees are suitable for different images, which particular times are auspicious for felling the tree, and how to propitiate the spirits who already dwell in the tree to find their habitation elsewhere, so that the tree may be free for the fresh habitation of the divinity to be shaped from it. Similar instructions and rites are set down for the selection and "neutralization" of stones to be used in the fashioning of images. In the Hindu plenum, every part of the order of "nature" may be the abode of a *genius loci*, so the first stage in claiming the raw material of an image is to invite those residents to depart.[79]

For the Indian artist, the *śilpin*, the creation of an image is, in part, a religious discipline. Entering into a state of concentration by means of yoga, the *śilpin* is to visualize the completed image in the mind's eye. According to the *śāstras*, the *śilpin*, before beginning a new work, undergoes a ritual purification and prays that he may successfully bring to form the divine image he has seen.

When an image is completed, there are special rites of consecration which take place, for the most part, in a specially consecrated booth outside the temple itself. First, the image is purified with a variety of ritually pure substances, such as *darbha* grass, honey, and ghee. Then by a rite called *nyāsa*, literally the "touching," various deities are established in different parts of the image: Brahmā in the chest, Indra in the hand, Sūrya in the eyes, the directional guardians in the ear, and so on. Thus, a particular image is symbolically inhabited by a number of deities, and the correspondences of the various parts of the iconic body to those deities is reminiscent of the correspondences between the body of the Primal Puruṣa and the deities created from him ("From his mind the moon was born, and from his eye the sun.")[80] Finally, *prāṇa* the "breathlife," is infused into the image in the central rite called *prāṇapratiṣṭhā*, "establishing the breathlife."[81] The infusion of *prāṇa* ordinarily takes the form of a *mantra* uttered by the ritually purified sponsor (*yajamāna*): "O Viṣṇu, approach this image and wake it up with thy embodiment of knowledge and the divine energies, which are concentrated in this one image."[82] The eyes of the image, which to this point have been sealed with a thick coat of honey and ghee, are now "opened" by the brahmin priest, who removes the coating with a golden needle.[83]

Jagannāth Deities

A striking example of the consecration of a new image is the periodic replacement of the Jagannāth images in the great temple of Kṛṣṇa Jagannāth in Purī in Orissa.[84] These are folk images, with their simple rectangular shape, their enormous eyes, and their stubby arms — all brightly painted. There is the black one, Kṛṣṇa; his brother Balarāma; and their sister Subhadrā. Every nineteen years,[85] these wood-carved images are replaced in a month-long rite called the "New Embodiment" (*navakalevara*). Taking a primary role in this "New Embodiment" are the temple servants, called *daitas*, whose association with these ancient autochthonous deities must be very ancient. First, the *daitas* organize a party, which includes brahmin priests, to go into the forest and select the proper trees from which the new images are to be made. Having selected each tree by looking for particular auspicious signs, the party performs the proper preliminary rites before the tree is cut. To begin with, the ground around the tree is seeded, and speedy germination is regarded as a good omen. For three days a *homa* fire is fed with oblations on the ground prepared by germination. Finally, the spirits of the tree are worshiped and asked to take their leave, and the tree is cut. The proper-sized log is hewn from the tree, wrapped in silk cloth, and pulled back to Purī in a wooden cart. The procession of carts, each bearing a log for one of the images, arrives at the temple compound, where a special shed has been constructed for the carving of the deities. The *daitas* carve the images according to ancient traditions passed down to them. For nearly two weeks they are at work, fashioning the images, and during this time the brahmin priests have already begun the extensive rites of consecration, called *pratiṣṭhā*. Since they cannot consecrate the images, which are still in the process of being made, they perform these intricate rites upon a substitute plug of wood from the log of each image. The rites of bathing, *nyāsa*, and fire oblations are performed with this plug of wood. When the new images are finished and brought inside the temple, a final and very dramatic rite of consecration takes place. In the middle of the night, the oldest of the *daitas*, with his eyes blindfolded and his hands wrapped with cloth, opens up the chest cavities of the old images and removes from each a small casket called the *brahmapadārtha*, the "Brahman substance." So sacred is this life substance that the old *daita* may neither see nor touch it. No one knows what it is. He places it into the hollow chest cavity of the new image, and plugs up the hole with the wood-plug which has substituted for the image in the long preparatory rites. The old images, their life-substance gone, are considered dead and are taken from the temple to a special burial ground where they are interred. After a period of mourning, the *daitas* paint the new images with their traditional bright colors. They do not, however, paint the pupils of the eyes upon the images. This, the final rite of the "New Embodiment," is performed by a brahmin priest. The images are then purified from their long contact with the servant-*daitas*. On the next day, they are taken out of the temple to be placed upon their grand processional chariots for the annual Rathyātrā festival. Hundreds of thousands of people fill the streets for the *darśan* of these new-born deities.

Although most images are established or consecrated with special rites to invoke the presence of the deity, some images are considered naturally sacred and do not need such rites. We have mentioned the *svarūpa* forms of Viṣṇu, such as the *śālagrāma* stone, and the *bāṇa liṅga* of Śiva. There are other images and *liṅgas*, however, made of quite ordinary substances, which are nonetheless considered to have appeared spontaneously, without the instrumental aid of a craftsman or a priest. They are said to be *svayambhū*, "self-born." According to their local traditions, they were simply discovered *in situ* — in the middle of a field or under a tree. A great number of India's most famous images are said to be "self-born," including the *liṅga* of Viśvanāth Śiva in Vārāṇasī, the image of Veṅkateśvara in Tirupati, and the image of Kṛṣṇa Śrīnāth-jī in Nāthdvārā.

D. Festivals and Images

Distinct from the ordinary worship and *darśan* of home and temple images, there are the special ways in which images are part of the festival celebrations of the yearly cycle. All over India, in great religious centers and in remote backcountry villages, the festivals of the sacred calendar are heralded by the appearance of special festival images. These images may be freshly painted on the whitewashed wall of one's home, such as the serpent (*nāga*) image which is painted by the doorway for the monsoon festival of Nāg Pañcamī. Or they may be clay images which one purchases in the bazaar, or great public images toward which one may make a donation.

The artists of the folk traditions have an important role in this seasonal image-making. For example, the women painters of Madhubāni in north Bihār produce elaborate and intricate art work on the clay walls of their homes, the themes usually determined by the festival season or the domestic ritual occasion. For weddings, they may paint auspicious designs on the bedroom wall of the new couple, or for festivals they may create an intricate geometric *maṇḍala* to designate the sacred space in front of the doorway or the altar of the home. In Vārāṇasī, the artisans produce small painted clay images which appear in the markets before certain festivals. For the birthday of Gaṇeśa, there will be thousands of plump, orange images of Gaṇeśa, for sale. At the time of Divālī, there will be images of the goddess Lakṣmī, who will be entreated in homes and shops for her auspicious blessings.

Kānchīpuram, Ekāmbareśvara temple, 16th century

For some festival occasions, large images of the gods are constructed under the sponsorship of a civic, religious, or educational institution. A wooden frame is filled out with straw, twine, and clay limbs, and is gaily painted. Bengal is famous for the images of the Devī which are made for the fall festival of Navarātri, the "Nine Nights" during which the Goddess is worshiped in her many forms. On the final night, the sponsoring group will take the image in procession to the river or to the seacoast and reverently, festively, sink the goddess-image in the waters. Similarly, in the famous Mahārāṣṭrian festival of Gaṇeśa Caturthī in the early fall, such images of Gaṇeśa are constructed. At the end of the festival, these images are carried to the seacoast in Bombay and sunk in the Arabian Sea. Such festivals dramatize the symbolic character of these images. For a few days it is consecrated to be the residence of the deity, and it is the focus of the people's *darśan*. When those days of celebration are over, the deities are given their leave and the corpse of the image is disposed of.

Another important ritual use of images is their public procession during great festivals. Here the usual roles are reversed: the deities come to the people and give them *darśan* in the streets. The images are brought out of the temple and, in a manner not unlike that of royalty, they travel by chariot or palanquin through the streets of town.

In the famous Rathyātrā festival at Purī, mentioned above, the Jagannāth deities are pulled in their enormous individual chariots down the wide processional street of Purī. This divine pilgrimage is a seven-day excursion from the great temple to a small summer residence at the far end of the street. Thousands put a hand to the long ropes which pull the chariots. While the Rathyātrā is perhaps the most famous festival procession, there are thousands of similar local processions. For example, on the full moon day at the beginning of the hot season in March/April, the Śrī Vaiṣṇavas of Madrās carry the images of Viṣṇu from their respective temples to the seashore, where all, including the deities, have a refreshing dip in the surf.

Sometimes the actual images from the temple sanctum are not processed in public, but smaller or duplicate images are taken out in procession. Such is the case in Madurai, where special *utsava mūrtis*, "festival images," of the Goddess Mīnākṣī and her divine

Lord Alagār, accompanied by brāhmin priest, approaches Madurai on horseback, borne on the shoulders of his devotees

consort Śiva Sundareśvara are carried in a royal palanquin through the streets. The Goddess reenacts her conquest of the world, her coronation as Queen, her marriage to Sundareśvara, and their marriage procession. This yearly festival, called Chittarai, coincides with another festival procession in which a local hill deity — Alagār, said to be a form of Viṣṇu — leaves his temple in the hills several days' journey south of Madurai and is carried in procession through the countryside toward Madurai, where he is to attend the yearly wedding of Mīnākṣī and Sundareśvara. Every year he is a day late for the wedding, but the real purpose of his journey through rural Tamilnād is apparently fulfilled in giving the people his public *darśan*.

CHAPTER 3

Image, Temple, and Pilgrimage

A. The Temple and the Image

THE CONSTRUCTION and consecration of a temple, according to the architectural portions of the *śilpaśāstras*, is very much like the shaping and consecration of an image. For example, the ground on which the temple is to be constructed is carefully selected on the basis of its auspicious situation and seeded for the auspicious sign of germination. Then the local *genii loci* who dwell in that ground are invited to leave and take up residence elsewhere: "Let spirits (*bhūta*), gods (*deva*), and demons (*rākṣasa*) depart and seek other habitations. From now on this place belongs to the divinity whose temples will be built here."[86] Finally, at the very end of the construction process, the "eyes" of the temple are opened by the master architect and the priestly architect, who ascend to the top of the temple in the middle of the night and pierce open the eyes of the temple with a golden needle. Is the temple also a divine image, as well as the abode of a divine image?

In building a temple, the universe in microcosm is reconstructed. The divine ground-plan is called a *maṇḍala*, a geometric map of the cosmos. At its center is the sanctum, where the image will be installed. Its eight directions are guarded by the cosmic regents called the *lokapālas*. Various planetary deities, world guardians, and gods are set in their appropriate quadrant. The temple is an architectural pantheon, with each portion of the structure inhabited by the gods.

The particular *maṇḍala* of the Hindu temple is called the *vāstu-puruṣa maṇḍala*. The Puruṣa is the cosmic "Person," from the sacrifice of whose giant body the entire universe was created, as told in Ṛg Veda X.90:

> From his mind the moon was born,
> and from his eye the sun,
> From his mouth Indra and the fire,
> From his breath the wind was born.
>
> From his navel arose the atmosphere,
> And from his head the sky evolved,
> From his feet the earth, and from his ear
> The cardinal points of the compass:
> So did they fashion forth these worlds.[87]

The body, as an organic whole diverse in the function of its parts and limbs, is here the image appropriated for the cosmos. The symbolic parallel between body and cosmos is articulated ritually in the construction of the Vedic fire altar, in which the body of Puruṣa (also called Prajāpati) is reconstructed from the various parts of the cosmos. A similar reconstruction of the body-cosmos occurs in the construction of the Hindu temple. The temple is the condensed image of the cosmos.

Stella Kramrisch, in explaining the meaning of the *vāstupuruṣa maṇḍala*, writes: "Puruṣa is the Universal Essence, the Principle of all things, the Prime Person whence all originates. Vāstu is the Site; in it Vāstu, bodily existence, abides; from it Vāstu derives its name. In bodily existence, Puruṣa, the Essence, becomes the Form. . . . Puruṣa himself has no substance. He gives it his impress. The substance is of wood, brick or stone in the temple."[88]

The building of a temple, like the shaping of an image, is not left to the creativity of the architect or craftsmen. It carefully follows canons of building and is, from beginning to end, a ritual activity. "From the stretching of the cord, or the drawing of the lines of the *maṇḍala*, every one of the movements is a rite and sustains, in its own sphere of effectiveness, the sacred building, to the same extent as the actual foundation supports its weight."[89]

A classical north India temple in the *nagara* style[90] is striking to the eyes of the Western observer in two ways: first, its exterior is teeming with intricately carved ornamentation and bas relief figures and, second, its interior sanctum is dark and usually windowless. The temple is said to be the architectural likeness of a mountain. Indeed, the various names of temple styles are the names of those great Himālayan peaks which are the home of the gods: Meru, Kailāsa, and Mandara. Both its lush exterior and its cavelike sanctum point to the symbolic linking of temple and mountain.

Kandarīya Mahādeva Temple, Khajurāho

The exterior of the temple, such as the temple of Kandarīya Mahādeva at Khajurāho, is a series of progressively higher porches or *maṇḍapas* culminating in the *śikhara*, the highest spire of the temple, situated directly over the inner sanctum. The word *śikhara* also means "mountain peak," and this temple-peak resembles a series of "foothills," the smaller *śikharas* massing, rising, one upon the other, toward their final culmination in the sun-disc, the *āmalaka*, the crowning cogged ring-stone at the very top of the temple.[91] Like the mountain, the temple links heaven and earth, and the sun-disc of the *āmalaka* is "the architectural symbol of the celestial world."[92]

Pilgrims come for the darśan of Mīnākṣī in Madurai

The prolixity of the cosmic mountain, covered with all forms of vegetative, animal, human, and divine life, is also replicated in the temple. As the sunlight changes through the day, the figures of every niche of the temple come alive. There are women applying cosmetics, warriors preparing for battle, gods and goddesses, serpent hooded *nāgas*, lions and elephants. The directional guardians stand forth in relief to protect this *maṇḍala*.

If the exterior of the temple is the articulation of the plenum of life, the interior of the temple directs our attention toward the center, the seed, the source of it all. The sanctum, approached through increasingly dim-lit porches, is the symbolic equivalent of the cave, deep within the mountain. The Kandarīya is literally the temple "Of the Cave."[93]

The sanctum of the temple is called the *garbhagṛha*, the "womb chamber." In this room, as the temple is being constructed, a rite called *garbhadhāna*, the "implanting of the seed," takes place. In the middle of the night, the priest plants the "seed" of the temple, in the form of a small casket which is set into the foundation.[94] It is this seed which symbolically germinates and grows directly upward, through the vertical shaft of the temple to the sky. The *garbhagṛha*, with its cave atmosphere, reminds us that there is a mystery, a secret, at the heart of this exuberant tradition of spirituality. The deep interior of the tradition is not flooded by the light of cathedral windows, but is deep within.

The journey of the worshiper to such a temple-mountain is a pilgrimage. Approaching the temple, one circumambulates it, symbolically attending to the entire visible world of name and form. Having seen all there is to see on the intricate exterior, one journeys to the interior, to the very center of the world. Often there is another circumambulatory passage around the *garbhagṛha*. Having made this final circumambulation, one receives the *darśan* of the deity at the center.

The temple is covered with artistic images, and it contains a primary consecrated image in its inner sanctum. In a larger sense, however, the temple *is* an image. It is not any particular deity, but the sacred *maṇḍala* of the cosmos as a whole. Kramrisch writes, "The temple is the concrete shape (*mūrti*) of the Essence; as such it is the residence and vesture of God. . . . The devotee who comes to the temple, to look at it, does so as a 'seer,' not as a spectator."[95]

B. Image and Pilgrimage

The same impulse for the *darśan* of the image which is at the center of the temple cultus also provides the impetus for pilgrimage. People go to "take the *darśan*" of the place and its deities, and to receive the *prasād* from its temples.

The most common term for such pilgrimage places is *tīrtha*, literally a "crossing place" or a "ford." The term originally referred to the ford in a river, where one could safely cross to the other shore.

The Bathing ghāṭs of Maṇikarṇikā, along the Gaṅgā at Kāśī

Through the centuries some of India's most important places of pilgrimage have indeed been located along the banks of her great rivers and have been "fords" in this geographical sense. As pilgrimage places, however, they are also symbolic and spiritual fords, where one may cross the flood of *saṁsāra*. Just as the "far shore" has become the predominant Indian image of the final spiritual destination of the soul's pilgrimage, so the "crossing place" has become an important image of the means of getting there.

The practice of pilgrimage, *tīrthayātrā*, has long been an important part of India's religious life. As early as the time of the epic Mahābhārata in the first two centuries C.E., *tīrthayātrā* was compared to the Vedic sacrifice in its benefits and, unlike the sacrifice, was a ritual activity accessible to all, not only to the very rich.[96]

In India today, the advent of modern means of transportation has served to stimulate the zeal for pilgrim travel. Pilgrimage is as popular and important a religious and cultural phenomenon as it was in the height of the Middle ages in Europe. The organization of pilgrim tours is a thriving business, and these *tīrthayātrās* in "deluxe" buses are advertised to include dozens of sacred sites on their itineraries.

Pilgrimage and Landscape

The entire land of India is, to the eyes of Hindu pilgrims, a sacred geography — from the Himālayas in the north to the tip of India at Cape Comorin in the south. As pilgrims circumambulate a temple, so do some pilgrims circumambulate the whole of this sacred land, including on their route the four *dhāms* or "abodes" of the divine at the four compass points: Badrīnāth in the north, Purī in the east, Rāmeśvaram in the south, and Dvārakā in the west. The names of the great mountain ranges, such as the Himālayas and the Vindhyas, and the names of the great rivers, such as the Gaṅgā, the Yamunā, the Narmadā, the Godāvarī, and the Kāverī — all are names that ring with mythological associations for Hindus. They are part of a very important symbolic geography which constitutes what Hindus mean by "India."

The Himālayas, for example, the "Abode of Snows," are also called *devālaya*, the "abode of the gods." Pilgrims have journeyed into the Himālayas for the *darśan* of great mountain peaks, such as Meru, the center of the world, Kailāsa, the home of Śiva, and Mandara, said to have been used as a churn to churn the Sea of Milk. They also seek the *darśan* of great Himālayan shrines, such as the Śaiva Kedārnāth, the Vaiṣṇava Badrīnāth, and the ice-*liṅga* at Amarnāth. The trek into the mountains has traditionally required great discipline and endurance and was often compared to the difficult austerities of ascetics and yogis.

The great Indian rivers, especially the Gaṅgā, have also been of symbolic importance. Himālayan pilgrims climb to the source of the River Gaṅgā Gaṅgotrī, where the river emerges from under a glacier. The Gaṅgā is called the River of Heaven and is said to have flowed in heaven alone before she agreed to come to earth. Śiva caught her in his tangled ascetic's hair to break the force of her fall, and from his head she flowed down through the Himālayas, leaving the mountains at Hardvār, also called Gaṅgādvār, "Door of the Gaṅgā," and from there flowing out upon the plains of India, past such great *tīrthas* as Prayāg and Vārāṇasī Kāśī, reaching the sea at Gaṅgā Sāgar on the Bay of Bengal. In Hindu hymns, the Gaṅgā is praised as a liquid form of Siva's divine energy, Śaktī.

The Himālayan shrine of Śiva as Kedārnāth

Bathing in the Gaṅgā is said to wash away all one's sins. The other sacred rivers of India are likened to the Gaṅgā in their purity and are often said to *be* the Gaṅgā, diverted miraculously to the various regions of India. All water used in ritual is symbolically transformed into sacred water by invoking the presence of the Gaṅgā and the other sacred rivers.

Sādhu at Bhaironāth, the shrine of protective deities on the hillside above Kedārnāth

While the Himālayas and the Gaṅgā are famous throughout India, there are hills, rivers, and mountains in the various regions of India which have their own sacred traditions. Regional pilgrimage — whether in Bengal, Mahārāṣṭra, or the Tamil south — has given a sense of unity and shared landscape to people of particular areas, language groups, or sectarian traditions. For example, the Śaiva *bhakti* tradition of Tamilnād has its own network of sacred shrines which link Tamil geography with the great deeds of Śiva Mahādeva. These places are praised in various *sthalapurāṇas*, "place-legends," as well as in the hymns of the Tamil *bhakti* poet-saints, the *nāyanmārs*, who flourished in the sixth to ninth centuries.[97] These saints were themselves perpetual pilgrims, wandering from place to place in Tamilnād and singing the praises of the various shrines of Śiva. Their poems praise Śiva as he dwells in each of these shrines: "... the God of Tōṇipuram where the sea has many beaches," or "... the coral-hued Lord who dwells in Kānūr of the fragrant groves."[98] The love of nature and the intimate knowledge of the particular hills, seashores, and fields of Tamilnād is evident in these poems, which inspire pilgrims not only to the love of Śiva, but to the love of the landscape where he lives.

Pilgrimage and Myth

In addition to pilgrimage places of geographical beauty, there are the many *tīrthas* associated with great events of the mythological tradition. India's myths are living in the geography of the land, and conversely India's geography is alive with mythology. The *tīrtha* is conceptually the counterpart of the *avatāra*, the word used to describe the divine "descents" of the gods. *Avatāra* comes from a variation of the *tīrtha* verbal root (*ava* + *tṛ*) meaning to "cross down," and precisely at those countless places where the gods have "crossed down" into this world as *avatāras* are the *tīrthas* where earthly pilgrims can make their spiritual crossings.

Some of the places especially famous for the mighty events which happened there include Kurukṣetra, the site of the great war of the Mahābhārata; Ayodhyā, the ancient capital of Lord Rāma; and Rāmeśvaram, where Rāma established a Śiva *liṅga* after crossing the sea to Laṅkā to rescue Sītā. Great centers, like Kāśī, seem to collect mythological traditions, to the extent that virtually all the great mythic events are associated with the city. Perhaps the best example of the direct linking of place and myth is in the area around Mathurā, the birthplace of Kṛṣṇa in central North India.

The land of Kṛṣna, called Vraj, covers an area of some sixty-four square miles in the area around Mathurā. Its spiritual center is in the village of Vṛndāvan. The area is filled with sites which mark the mythic events of the life of Kṛṣṇa, from his birthplace in Mathurā, to the home of the baby Kṛṣṇa's foster parents in Gokul and the later childhood home of Kṛṣṇa in Vṛndāvan. The places of Kṛṣṇa's divine "play" (*līlā*) amidst the pastoral cowherding folk of Vraj are called *līlāsthalas*, the "places of the Lord's play."[99] There is the holy hill of Govardhan, which young Kṛṣṇa is said to have lifted with one finger; there is the pool where his beloved Rādhā is said to have bathed; there is the tree by the river where Kṛṣṇa hung the clothes he stole from the milkmaids, the *gopīs*, as they bathed; and there is the grove where Kṛṣṇa and the *gopīs* danced in the middle of the night. Countless such *līlāsthalas*, associated with even the most minute details of Kṛṣṇa's life, have created a sacred landscape as intricate as that of medieval Palestine, where such sites as the place where Mary nursed Jesus, the place where Mary washed Jesus' clothes, and the place where the food was cooked to be served at the Last Supper, were located with imaginative precision.[100] In Vraj, these many places are said to bear the "traces" (*cihna*) of Kṛṣṇa, and they bid the pilgrim to constant remembrance of him and his miraculous life. While the pilgrim to Vraj may visit the temples of Vṛndāvan and Mathurā for the *darśan* of the various images of Kṛṣṇa, the real power of Vraj pilgrimage is in the land of Vraj itself. Pilgrims undertake a special pilgrimage through the rural countryside of Vraj, visiting the groves, the pools, and the hillocks where Kṛṣṇa's "traces" may be found. The earth itself is said to be holy here. The "dust of Vraj," (*Vraj ki raj*) is considered sanctified by the feet of Kṛṣṇa, and pilgrims touch it reverently to their foreheads.

Pilgrimage and the Sacred Image

There are other *tīrthas* in which primary importance is attached to the particular *image* of the deity which is found there, and not so much to the place itself or to its mythological associations. For example, pilgrims go to the sacred hill of Tirupati in Andhra Pradesh especially for the *darśan* of Śrī Veṅkaṭeśvara, an ancient icon said to be a form of Viṣṇu.[101] In Mahārāṣṭra, the twice-yearly pilgrimage of the Vārkarī sect to Paṇḍharpur is also oriented toward the *darśan* of a particular deity, Viṭhobā, who is said to be a form of Kṛṣṇa.[102] According to legend, the Lord came to bless a particular devotee who was faithful in his duties toward his parents. The devotee did not even take time from his filial duties to greet the Lord properly, but simply threw him a brick to stand on. Kṛṣṇa, impressed with such devotion, has remained standing there ever since.

Another icon of great renown is the cultic image of Kṛṣṇa as the Lord of Mt. Govardhan in Vraj. The image is not even in Vraj, however, but is in Nāthdvārā in Rājasthān. According to the Vallabhite sectarian tradition, the Lord appeared out of Govardhan in a spontaneously formed image called Śrīnāth-jī.[103] They served this icon of Kṛṣṇa in Vraj, and when Muslim persecution forced them to abandon Vraj, they took the icon westward and ultimately built a temple to house it in the Arāvalli Hills. The place, called Nāthdvārā, is visited by Vallabhite pilgrims solely for the purpose of having Śrīnāth-jī's *darśan*.

Finally, we should again mention the unique wooden images of Kṛṣṇa Jagannāth, Balarāma, and Subhadrā housed in the great temple complex at Purī. The cultus of Jagannāth, like that of all of the above mentioned images, has an antiquity which extends deep into the regional folk traditions.[104] Since the specifically Vaiṣṇava identity of these images is attached to a more ancient cultus, it is little wonder that the stories of Kṛṣṇa have little importance in Purī. The myths associated with this place are, rather, those which concern the appearance of these images, which are said to have been carved by the craftsman of the gods, Viśvakarman, from a log washed ashore in the time of the legendary king Indradyumna.[105] Here, as in many Indian temples with a strong regional affiliation, the day to day service of the deities in the temple is parallel in structure to the honor and service which the king used to receive.

Pilgrimage and the Saints

When the Tamil pilgrims walk to a distant Śiva shrine singing the songs composed by one of the *nāyanmār* poets over one thousand years ago, they join in a tradition which links them with the saints as well as with the sacred shrines. All over India, the *bhakti* movements emphasized the direct, devotional love of God. For some, such as Kabīr in the north and Basavanna in the south, this direct love meant a diminished regard for the elaborate brahmanical temple cult and for the great ritual centers of pilgrimage. God, after all, is close within the heart. For most of the *bhakti* saints, however, especially those who saw the Lord as intensely personal and endowed with qualities (*saguṇa*), the image-incarnations of the Lord were of great imprtance and became the focal point of their devotion. The saints sang their hymns at the doors of the temples, and so did the pilgrims who followed them. The Śrī Vaiṣṇavas went to Tirupati and Śrī Raṅgam. The Śaiva Siddhāntins went to Kāñcī and Cidambaram. The Gaudīya Vaiṣṇavas went to Vṛndāvan.

The saints themselves were often great pilgrims and wanderers. Many took up a life of homelessness, becoming itinerant minstrels and poets. The people of the *bhakti* movements which these saints launched have followed the footsteps of the saints in pilgrimage. In Mahārāṣṭra, for example, the Vārkarī pilgrims who journey to Paṇḍharpur bring the great Mahārāṣṭrian saints along on pilgrimage with them. Traveling in processional groups from their own districts, the pilgrims follow after a cart which carries the *pādukās*, "footprints," of one of the great saints, such as Tukāraṁ, Eknāth, or Jñāneśvara. The most famous of these processions follows the *pādukas* of Jñāneśvara, starting from a village near Poona and traveling over 150 miles to Paṇḍharpur. On the way, they sing the songs of the Mahārāṣṭrian saints, who made this journey many times:

> I should like to become the small pebbles
> or the big stones, or the dust
> of the road which leads to Paṇḍharpur.
> Thus would I be under the feet of the Saints.[106]

While the pilgrims to Paṇḍharpur travel with the saints, they also travel *to* the saints, for two of the beloved Mahārāṣṭrian saints, Nāmdev and Cokhāmela, are interred right at the doorstep of Viṭhobā's temple. Worshiping the saints is part of the pilgrimage to Paṇḍharpur.[107] Elsewhere in India, pilgrimage to places associated with the saints, especially their tombs or *samādhis*, is not uncommon. A striking example is the annual pilgrimage to the tomb of the Rājput hero-saint Rāmdev, which attracts thousands of pilgrim' from Rājasthān, Mahārāṣṭra, and Gujarāt each year.

The saints (*sants*) are not the same as the *sādhus*, the "holy men." Perhaps the most notable distinction between them is that the saints of the *bhakti* movements were, to a great extent, anti-establishment figures who often championed the downtrodden and the untouchables and despised brahmanical ritualism, while the *sādhus* and *sannyāsins* represent the brahmanical establishment, even in transcending it by casting off their worldly *dharma*. Nonetheless, the notion that there is something to be gained from the presence and *darśan* of a holy person is equally relevant to both saints and *sādhus*. Just as pilgrims follow the saints, so do they follow the *sādhus*.

Hindus seek the *darśan* of *sādhus* and *sannyāsins* who tend to congregate at the great *tīrthas*, such as Kāśī, Hardvār, and Badrīnāth.

In a sense, these renouncers are the patrons of *tīrthas* and serve to enhance the popularity and power of the *tīrtha* by their very presence.[108] In the Bhāgavata Purāṇa, King Yudhiṣṭhira emphasizes this point in speaking to a sage who has just returned from a pilgrimage: "Devotees like you, who have become *tīrthas* themselves, are the ones who make the *tīrthas* into crossing places by embodying the presence of God there."[109]

Darśan at Mṛtuñjaya Temple, Banāras

The term *tīrtha* refers not only to places, but may also refer to people — holy people who have themselves become "crossings." In the ancient Jain tradition, the spiritual pathfinders were called *tīrthāṅkaras*, "ford-makers." Much later, one of the orders of *sādhus* organized by Śaṅkara took the name *tīrtha* as a title. The point is clear enough: holy men can also help one reach the "far shore." Thus, in going to geographical *tīrthas*, Hindus have had a special preference for those places where the walking-*tīrthas* congregate.

Pilgrimage Place as Divine Image

Just as the temple may become an image of the sacred whole of the cosmos, so do some *tīrthas* become images of the cosmos. The place becomes an icon.

A direct parallel to the structure of a temple may be seen in the city of Madurai in Tamilnād, where the city is laid out in the shape of a *maṇḍala*. At the center is the temple compound of Mīnākṣī and Sundareśvara, with its tall, elaborately carved gateways, called *gopurams*, in the four directions. Around the temple are three concentric square processional streets. Here an entire city has been built according to the plan of the *śilpaśāstras*, and the plan is precisely that of the *vāstupuruṣa maṇḍala* which delimits the sacred space of a temple.[110] The city is the cosmos, bounded from forces of disorder by the boundaries of order which the *maṇḍala* establishes. Each year, in the Chittarai festival, the Goddess Mīnākṣī reestablishes the sacred order by conquering the lords of the eight directions and by establishing the sovereignty of herself and Śiva Sundareśvara at the center of this cosmos.

The city of Vārāṇasī, acknowledged by Hindus as a whole to be the most sacred of the *tīrthas*, is also a sacred image of the cosmos. The city is said to be the permanent earthly home of Lord Śiva, and it is often called Avimukta, the "Never-Forsaken," the place Śiva never leaves. According to myth, Śiva upholds this city on the tip of his trident even during the *pralaya* when the universal flood destroys the earth.[111] And from this place the world is created again. The city is also called Kāśī, the "City of Light." It is here, according to myth, that Śiva's fiery *liṅga* of light burst up from the netherworlds, split open the earth, and rose to pierce through the top of the highest heavens — a luminous, fathomless, *axis mundi*. Moreover, Kāśī is not only the location of that mythic episode, but is said to *be* that *liṅga* itself. The entire city, a sacred circle or *maṇḍala* with a radius of ten miles, is said to be a *liṅga* — the very embodiment of Śiva.

With its three thousand years of continuous habitation, Kāśī's *maṇḍala* is hardly as ordered as that of Madurai. Nonetheless, the elements of the whole are here. The eight directions are said to have originated in Kāśī, receiving their respective realms of sovereignty by establishing Śiva *liṅgas* in Kāśī. Similarly the heavenly deities who govern time are said to have received jurisdiction over time in Kāśī. The temples of all these deities, in addition to the temples of

Mīnākṣī Temple Complex, Madurai, Tamilnādu, 17th century

Viṣṇu, Durgā, Bhairava, Gaṇeśa, and all the gods, have their places within the patterns of Kāśī's sacred geography. At the center is the famous *liṅga* of Viśvanāth — Śiva as "Lord of the Universe." The whole of the city is protected by a grid of fifty-six Gaṇeśas, who sit at the eight compass points in seven concentric circles spreading outward from Viśvanāth.

As a microcosm, Kāśī is said to contain all the *tīrthas* of India's sacred geography within her borders. Thus, in the city of Kāśī there are temples, tanks, lakes, and rivulets which represent the symbolic presence of such places as Kedārnāth and Badrīnāth in the Himālayas, Kāñcī and Rāmeśvaram in the Tamil south, Purī in the east, Dvārakā in the west, the old cities of Mathurā, Ayodhyā, and Ujjain, the Narmadā and Godāvarī rivers, the Vindhya and Himālaya mountains.

In Kāśī, the whole of the sacred world is gathered together into one place. The sacred landscape of India is here. The great myths of the tradition are said to have happened here. There is a great density of images and *liṅgas* here. And there has always been a great congregation of saints, *sādhus*, and *sannyāsins* here.

Although Kāśī condenses the entire universe in its microcosm, it is also said to transcend the entire universe. It is well known as that *tīrtha* which enables those who die within its borders to make the final "crossing" from this shore of birth and death to the "far shore" of *moksa*. It is believed that to die in Kāśī is to gain liberation. Thus, while ordinary pilgrims may come to Kāśī with many of the same vows and desires they bring to other *tīrthas*, there is another group of pilgrims who come to Kāśī to stay and to live out their years until they die. For them, this is the destination at the end of the pilgrim road. It brings to an end not only the circuit of pilgrimage in India, but the long soul's pilgrimage through life after life.

Notes

1. Victor and Edith Turner, *Image and Pilgrimage in Christian Culture* (New York: Columbia University Press, 1978). See especially Chapter 4, "Iconophily and Iconoclasm in Marian Pilgrimage."

2. Agehananda Bharati, *The Ochre Robe* (New York: Doubleday and Co., Inc., 1970), p. 161.

3. Charlotte Vaudeville, conversation, April 1980.

4. Bhagavad Gītā 11.8.

5. Jan Gonda, *Eye and Gaze in the Veda* (Amsterdam: North-Holland Publishing Company, 1969).

6. Such an instance is cited in Margaret Stevenson, *The Rites of the Twice-Born* (1920, reprint ed., New Delhi: Oriental Books, 1971), p. 414.

7. In the Jagannāth deities, Kṛṣṇa is the black one on the right; his brother Balarāma is white and is on the left; their sister Subhadrā is yellow and is between them. See II.C below for a description of their creation and consecration.

8. Stella Kramrisch, *The Hindu Temple*, 2 vols. (1946, reprint ed., Delhi: Motilal Banarsidass, 1976), p. 136.

9. Gonda, *Eye and Gaze in the Veda*, p. 19.

10. Daniel H. H. Ingalls, *Sanskrit Poetry from Vidyākara's "Treasury"* (Cambridge: Harvard University Press, 1965), p. 138 ff.

11. Ingalls, p. 138.

12. Gonda, *Eye and Gaze in the Veda*, p. 4.

13. Cited in Gonda, *Eye and Gaze in the Veda*, p. 9.

14. Jan Gonda, *The Vision of the Vedic Poets* (The Hague: Mouton & Co., 1963), p. 28.

15. Gonda, *The Vision of the Vedic Poets*, p. 25.

16. E. M. Forster, *A Passage to India* (1924, reprint, Harmondsworth, England: Penguin Books Limited, 1974), p. 288.

17. Rudolf Arnheim, *Visual Thinking* (Berkeley: University of California Press, 1969), p. 3.

18. Susan Sontag, *On Photography* (New York: Farrar, Straus and Giroux, 1977).

19. Sontag, p. 115.

20. Arnheim, Chapter 2, "The Intelligence of Visual Perception."

21. Gonda, *The Vision of the Vedic Poets*, Chapter I, "Introduction" and Chapter II, "'*Dhih*' in the Ṛg Veda."

22. Susanne K. Langer, *Philosophy in a New Key*, 3rd edition (Cambridge: Harvard University Press, 1942), p. 145.

23. Arnheim, p. 19.

24. Arnheim, Chapter 5, "The Past in the Present" and Chapter 6, "The Images of Thought."

25. Arnheim, p. 278.

26. Sontag, p. 93.

27. William Foster, ed., *Early Travels in India 1583-1619* (London: Oxford University Press, 1921), p. 23.

28. M. A. Sherring, *The Sacred City of the Hindus* (London: Trubner & Co., 1868), p. 37.

29. Mark Twain, *Following the Equator* (Hartford, Connecticut: The American Publishing Company, 1898), p. 504.

30. Arnheim, p. 5.

31. Arnheim, p. 12.

32. Edward C. Sachau, ed., *Alberuni's India* (Delhi: S. Chand & Co., 1964), p. 17.

33. Theodore Roszak, *Where the Wasteland Ends* (Garden City, New York: Doubleday & Co., 1972), Chapter 4, "The Sin of Idolatry."

34. U. R. Anantha Murthy, "Search for an Identity: A Viewpoint of a Kannada Writer," in Sudhir Kakar, ed., *Identity and Adulthood* (Delhi: Oxford University Press, 1979), pp. 109-110.

35. James Hillman, *Re-Visioning Psychology* (New York: Harper & Row, 1975), pp. xiv-xv, 158-9.

36. E. M. Forster, *A Passage to India*, p. 135.

37. Mark Twain, *Following the Equator*, p. 397.

38. Francis G. Hutchins, *The Illusion of Permanence* (Princeton: Princeton University Press, 1967), p. 142.

39. The hierarchical model is the one adopted by Louis Dumont in *Homo Hierarchicus* (Chicago: University of Chicago Press, 1970).

40. Betty Heimann, *Facets of Indian Thought* (London: George Allen & Unwin, 1964), pp. 21-22.

41. Bṛhadāraṇyaka Upaniṣad 3.9.1. Quoted here from Robert E. Hume, *The Thirteen Principal Upaniṣads* (1877, 2nd ed. revised, London: Oxford University Press, 1931).

42. From the "Nārāyaṇīstuti" in the *Devī Māhātmya* of the *Mārkaṇḍeya Purāṇa*. Quoted in Kramrisch, *The Hindu Temple*, p. 298.

43. Heimann, p. 33.

44. J. N. Banerjea, *The Development of Hindu Iconography* (3rd edition, Delhi: Munshiram Manoharlal, 1974), Chapter II, "The Antiquity of Image-Worship in India." There is some controversy about the existence of images in Vedic times, centering around a verse "Who will buy this my Indra for ten cows?" — Ṛg Veda IV.24.10. Banerjea discusses the matter here.

45. Ananda Coomaraswamy, *Yakṣas*, 2 vols., (1928-1931, reprinted in one volume, New Delhi: Munshiram Manoharlal, 1971), especially Part II, "Water Cosmology," pp. 13-17.

46. Charlotte Vaudeville, "Braj, Lost and Found," *Indo-Iranian Journal* 18 (1976), p. 199. See also Vaudeville, "The Govardhan Myth in Northern India," *Indo-Iranian Journal* 22 (1980).

47. The Abbé J. A. Dubois, *Hindu Manners, Customs and Ceremonies* (3rd edition, Oxford: The Clarendon Press, 1906), p. 631.

48. Stella Kramrisch, *Indian Sculpture* (London: Oxford University Press, 1933), plate IX, no. 36.

49. For the hierophany of the fiery *liṅga* see Liṅga Purāṇa 17.6—19.17; Śiva Purāṇa, Vidyeśvara Saṁhitā, 6-10. These two Purāṇas are translated into English in the *Ancient Indian Tradition and Mythology* Series, J. L. Shastri, ed.

50. Charlotte Vaudeville, conversation, April 1980. Since the trident is also one of Śiva's characteristic weapons, many associate it primarily with him. According to Vaudeville, the trident, on the contrary, is almost invariably an indication of the *devī*.

51. V. S. Apte, *Sanskrit-English Dictionary*, 3 vols. (Poona: Prasad Prakashan, 1957).

52. See the work of Ananda Coomaraswamy, *Yakṣas*; V. S. Agrawal, *Ancient Indian Folk Cults* (Vārāṇasī: Prithivi Prakashan, 1970); and F. D. K. Bosch, *The Golden Germ* (Gravenhage: Mouton & Co., 1960).

53. From the Mauryan period there is the *yakṣa* from Parkham (Mathurā Museum), the *yakṣa* from Patna (Calcutta, Indian Museum), and the *yakṣī* from Besnagar (Calcutta, Indian Museum). For plates of the first two, see Benjamin Rowland, *The Art and Architecture of India* (1953, 3rd revised edition, Baltimore, Md.: Penguin Book, 1967), plates 24 & 25.

54. Rowland, pp. 221-227.

55. See Rowland, Chapter 17, "The Period of the Hindu Dynasties."

56. See Ananda Coomaraswamy's classic essay on "The Dance of Śiva" in *The Dance of Śiva: Fourteen Indian Essays* (1918, reprint New York: Farrar Straus & Co., 1957).

57. Heimann, Chapter II, "Visible Thought."

58. Cited in Albert C. Moore, *Iconography of Religions, An Introduction* (Philadelphia: Fortress Press, 1977), p. 243.

59. I think especially here of the older Hindi film *Sampūrṇa Tīrthayātrā*, the tale of a woman who gets her husband back by undertaking a circumambulatory pilgrimage of India. Śiva is portrayed quite dramatically, as he engineers it all from his Himālayan abode.

60. The Hindi film of the *Viṣṇu Purāṇa* included this scene of the churning of the Sea of Milk.

61. *Viṣṇu Saṁhitā* XXIX.55-57. Cited in L. A. Ravi Varma, "Rituals of Worship" in H. Bhattacharya, ed. *The Cultural Heritage of India*, Vol. IV (1937, 2nd edition Calcutta: Ramakrishna Mission Institute of Culture, 1956), p. 453.

62. Jābāladarśana Upaniṣad 3.59. Paṇḍita Jagadīśa Śastri, ed., *Upaniṣatsangraha* (Delhi: Motilal Banarsidass, 1970).

63. Banerjea, p. 80.

64. John B. Carman, *The Theology of Rāmānuja* (New Haven: Yale University Press, 1974), pp. 180-81.

65. Carman, Chapter 5, "Paratva and Saulabhya as Interpretive Concepts."

66. *Śrimād Bhagavadgītā* with the commentary of Rāmānuja and a Hindi translation (Gorakhpur: Gita Press, 1968), p. 144.

67. J. A. B. Van Buitenen, *Rāmānuja on the Bhagavadgītā* (Delhi: Motilal Banarsidass, 1968), p. 78.

68. Bharatan Kumarappa, *The Hindu Conception of the Deity as Culminating in Rāmānuja* (London: Luzac and Company, 1934), pp. 316-317.

69. This part of the *Bhagavadgītā Bhāsya* of Rāmānuja is quoted here as cited by Kumarappa, p. 316.

70. Bhagavad Gītā 2.58.

71. See P. V. Kane, *History of Dharmaśāstra,* Vol. II, Part II (2nd edition, reprinted Poona: Bhandakar Oriental Research Institute, 1974), pp. 716-717.

72. *Nityakarma Vidhi tathā Devapūjā Paddhati* (Vārāṇasī: Ratnadās Surekā, 1976).

73. *Ibid.*

74. T. A. G. Rao, *Elements of Hindu Iconography*, Vol. II, Part II (1914, reprinted Delhi: Motilal Banarsidass, 1968), pp. 77-78.

75. The *śilpaśāstras* include such specifically artistic texts as the Viṣṇudharmottara Purāṇa and the *Manasāra śilpaśāstra*; texts which treat artistic topics in part, such as the *Bṛhatsaṁhitā;* and sections of major Purāṇas, such as the Matsya, Bhaviṣya, and Agni Purāṇas.

76. Rao, Vol. II, Part II deals entirely with the various forms of Śiva.

77. Banerjea, p. 82.

78. Śukracārya, cited in Ananda Coomaraswamy, *The Transformation of Nature in Art* (1934, reprinted New York: Dover Publications, Inc. 1956), p. 167.

79. For the texts describing the selection of the wood, see Banerjea, pp. 204 ff., and for the descriptions of the selection of stone, see Banerjea, pp. 217 ff.

80. Ṛg Veda X.90.

81. For a description of *prāṇapratiṣṭhā,* see Kane, *History of Dharmaśāstra,* Vol. II, Part II, Chapter 26.

82. Agni Purāṇa 60. There is an English translation of the *Agni Purāṇa* by M. N. D. Shastri, (Vārāṇasī: Chowkhamba Sanskrit Series Office, 1967).

83. Matsya Purāṇa 264.32-34. See J. D. Akhtar, ed., *The Matsya Purāṇa,* Sacred Books of the Aryans Series, Vol. I (Delhi: Oriental Publishers, 1972).

84. For my introduction to the rites of the Navakalevara I am indebted to Frédérique Marglin. The rites are described in G. C. Tripathi, "Navakalevara: The Unique Ceremony of the 'birth' and the 'death' of the 'Lord of the World'" in

Anncharlott Eschmann, Hermann Kulke, and G. C. Tripathi, eds., *The Cult of Jagannāth and the Regional Tradition of Orissa* (Delhi: Manohar, 1978). This excellent book contains essays by each of the editors on the history and the nature of the cult of Jagannāth in relation to the folk traditions of Orissa.

85. The Navakalevara is performed every 19 years or every 12 years. It is performed only in a year in which there are *two* months of Āṣāḍha, one being the extra month added to the calendar every 32 months to compensate for the fact that lunar months are somewhat shorter than solar months. Āṣāḍha is the summer month (June/July) when the Rathayātrā takes place and the extra month is the time used to create the new images.

86. Kramrisch, *The Hindu Temple*, p. 13.

87. R. C. Zaehner, trans. *Hindu Scriptures* (London: J. M. Dent & Sons, Ltd., 1966), pp. 8-10.

88. Kramrisch, *The Hindu Temple*, pp. 6-7. Kramrisch's work, which is certainly the major work on the Hindu temple, is in its entirety an exploration of the temple as *vāstupuruṣa maṇḍala*.

89. Kramrisch, *The Hindu Temple*, p. 39.

90. Rowland, pp.276, 280 explains the *nagara* style of temple, as distinguished from the *drāviḍa* and *vesara* styles. Essentially, the *nagara* is the north Indian, post-Gupta temple, with the distinctive *śikhara* over the sanctum.

91. Kramrisch, *The Hindu Temple*, pp. 348-356, ("The Āmalaka").

92. Kramrisch, *The Hindu Temple*, p. 351.

93. Kramrisch, *The Hindu Temple*, p. 365.

94. Kramrisch, *The Hindu Temple*, p. 165.

95. Kramrisch, *The Hindu Temple*, p. 165.

96. Vishnu S. Sukthankar (and others), editors, *Mahābhārata*, 19 vols. (Poona: Bhandarkar Oriental Research Institute, 1933-1959), 3.80. 34-38.

97. See George W. Spencer, "The Sacred Geography of the Tamil Shaivite Hymns," *Numen*, Vol. XVII.3 (December1970), pp. 232-244. There is also an excellent unpublished paper by Indira Peterson, "Singing of a Place: Pilgrimage as Metaphor and Motif in the *Tēvāram* Songs of the Tamil Saivite Saints," presented at the Southern Asian Institute, Columbia University, March 4, 1980. I am indebted to Indira Peterson for sending me a copy of this paper.

98. These verses, respectively by Appar and Campantar, are cited in Indira Peterson, "Singing of a Place ...," p. 7.

99. For the *līlāsthalas* of Vraj, see Charlotte Vaudeville, "Braj, Lost and Found," cited above.

100. Perhaps the most entrancing of the medieval pilgrim narratives on the *līlāsthalas* of Palestine is Felix Fabri, *The Book of the Wanderings of Brother Felix Fabri*, tr. A. Stewart, (London: Palestine Pilgrims Text Society, Vol. X, 1887-97).

101. See P. Sitapati, *Śrī Veṅkaṭeśvara, The Lord of the Seven Hills, Tirupati* (Bombay: Bharatiya Vidya Bhavan, 1972).

102. See Charlotte Vaudeville, "Paṇḍharpūr, The City of Saints," in H. Buck and G. Yocum, eds. *Structural Approaches to South India Studies* (Chambersburg, PA: Anima Publications, 1973). There is also a monograph on Paṇḍharpur by G. A. Deleury, *The Cult of Viṭhobā* (Poona: Deccan College, 1960). Vaudeville's article, although shorter, gives a clearer picture of the complex layering of folk traditions in Paṇḍharpur.

103. See Charlotte Vaudeville, "The Govardhan Myth in North India," part II, "The Manifestation of Śrī Govardhannāthjī in the Vallabhite Tradition," *Indo-Iranian Journal* 22 (1980).

104. See Anncharlott Eschmann, "Hinduization of Tribal Deities in Orissa: The Śākta and Śaiva Typology," and "The Vaiṣṇava Typology of Hinduization and the Origin of Jagannātha" in Eschmann, et. al., eds., *The Cult of Jagannāth and the Regional Tradition of Orissa.*

105. The story of Indradyumna is told in the *Skanda Purāṇa, Vaiṣṇava Khanda, Puruṣottama Māhātmya*, chapters 18 and 19.

106. Deleury, p. 76. This particular *abhaṅga* is Tukārām's.

107. Vaudeville, "Paṇḍharpūr: City of Saints," pp. 158-159.

108. A. Bharati, "Pilgrimage Sites and Indian Civilization," in J. W. Elder, ed., *Chapters in Indian Civilization*, Vol. I (Dubuque: Kendall Hunt Publishing Company, 1970), p. 90.

109. Bhāgavata Purāṇa I.13.10. C. L. Goswami, tr., *Śrīmad Bhāgavata Mahāpurāṇa* [With Sanskrit text and English translation], (Gorakhpur: The Gita Press, 1971).

110. Julian S. Smith, *Madurai, India: The Architecture of a City* (Cambridge: M.I.T. Master of Architecture Thesis, 1976).

111. See Diana L. Eck, *Banāras, City of Light* (New York: Alfred A. Knopf, 1982), Chapter 7, "City of All India."

APPENDIX I

Bibliography

I. General

Babb, Lawrence A. *The Divine Hierarchy: Popular Hinduism in Central India.* (New York: Columbia University Press, 1975). An introduction to Hinduism in its popular setting, with attention to the relation between the brahmanical and the folk traditions. Sections on *pūjā*, the weekly, monthly, and yearly festival round, and the rites of the life cycle. A final section on the "hierarchy" of the deities of the pantheon. A very readable ethnography for beginning students.

Dimmitt, Cornelia and J. A. B. Van Buitenen, eds., and trans. *Classical Hindu Mythology: A Reader in the Sanskrit Purāṇas.* (Philadelphia: Temple University Press, 1978). An introduction to the popular myths of the tradition, including sections on creation, Śiva, Viṣṇu, Kṛṣṇa, the Goddess, and others. A few selections on pilgrimage as well. A taste of Purāṇic literature, with good introductions to each topic.

Lannoy, Richard. *The Speaking Tree: A Study of Indian Culture and Society.* (London: Oxford University Press, 1971). A general introduction to India, including sections on family, social structure, values. The first section, however, "The Aesthetic Factor in Indian History," attempts to introduce India and give a sense of the movement of its history by focusing on the development of art, architecture, and image, from the Indus Valley to the Muslim period. This is an especially bold attempt and is recommended for that reason.

Moore, Albert C. *Iconography of Religions: An Introduction.* (Philadelphia: Fortress Press, 1977). A general introduction to the use of images in religion, with sections on each of the religious communities and their attitudes toward and use of images. Includes sections on primal, Greek and Egyptian religious images; the Hindu, Buddhist, and Jain traditions; East Asia; and the prophetic iconoclastic traditions of the West.

II. The Nature of the Hindu Image

Coomaraswamy, Ananda. *The Transformation of Nature in Art.* (1934, reprint New York: Dover Press, 1956). An attempt to develop an Asian theory of art and aesthetics. A final chapter on the "Origin and Use of Images in India."

The Dance of Śiva (1918, reprint New York: Farrar Straus & Co., 1957). The title essay of this collection of fourteen essays is an excellent interpretive piece on the "Dance of Śiva" and is very readable.

Banerjea, J. N. *The Development of Hindu Iconography.* (2nd revised edition 1956, reprint New Delhi: Munshiram Manoharlal, 1974). A classic introduction to Hindu iconography, with excellent sections on the origin and development of image worship in India. Later sections on cult icons, including Viṣṇu and Sūrya, Śiva and Śakti. A standard work.

Rao, T.A.G. *Elements of Hindu Iconography,* 2 vols., each of 2 parts. (1914, 2nd edition, Delhi: Motilal Banarsidass, 1968). An earlier work than Banerjea's, but still a classic guide to the various images of the Hindu pantheon.

Rowland, Benjamin. *The Art and Architecture of India: Hindu, Buddhist, Jain.* (1953, 3rd revised edition, Baltimore: Penguin Books, 1967). An historical survey of the development of art and architecture in India.

III. Image, Temple, and Pilgrimage

Bhardwaj, S. M. *Hindu Pilgrimage in India.* (Berkeley: University of California Press, 1973). A general introduction to pilgrimage in India, based on the Epic and Purāṇic sources. A special focus on the Hardvār region and the adjacent Himālayan area in north India. The work of a geography scholar, but of use for students of religion.

Eck, Diana L. *Banaras, City of Light.* (New York: Alfred A. Knopf, 1982). A study of the sacred city of Banāras (also Kāśī, Vārāṇasī) with attention to its gods, temples, and sacred geography.

Hawley, John S. with Śrīvatsa Goswāmi. *At Play with Krishna.* (Princeton: Princeton University Press, 1981). A translation of several of the popular dramas, called *līlās,* which are performed during seasons of pilgrimage in Vṛndāvan in the land of Kṛṣṇa in rural north India. The *līlās* focus on well known and loved events of the life of Kṛṣṇa, and the introduction provided to the *līlās* and the book as a whole sets this aspect of Kṛṣṇa *bhakti* in its living context.

Kramrisch, Stella. *The Hindu Temple,* 2 vols. (1946, reprint, Delhi: Motilal Banarsidass, 1976). A great classic on the temple, its conception and articulation as a *vāstu maṇḍala.* An introductory section on the temple-*tīrtha* correspondences. Based primarily on the north Indian *naagara* style temples of Khajurāho and Bhuvaneśvar.

Michell, George. *The Hindu Temple: An Introduction to its Meaning and Forms.* (New York: Harper and Row, 1977). A more introductory work than Kramrisch's. Part I summarizes some of the meanings of the temple, drawing heavily upon Kramrisch. Part II reviews the forms of the temple in various parts of India and Southeast Asia, with photographs and ground plans.

APPENDIX II

Note on Pronunciation

The text contains both Sanskrit and Hindi words and names, as well as a few from the Tamil South. Certain words and names I have spelled in Hindi, simply because they are so much a part of the people's tradition that it would be archaic for the student to learn these terms primarily in Sanskrit. Thus, I have used *darśan*, *prasād*, and *āśram* rather than the Sanskrit *darśana*, *prasāda*, and *āśrama*. Similarly, I used the names *Jagannāth*, *Vṛndāvan*, and *Govardhan* rather than *Jagannātha*, *Vṛndāvana*, and *Govardhana*. I have kept in Sanskrit transliteration the names of the gods, rites, and concepts which a student will commonly meet in other reading.

1. There are short and long vowels, the latter indicated by "long-marks" or macrons. Here are some examples from this text:

a	(as in but) *darśan*	*ā*	*(as in father) prasād*
i	(as in it) *liṅga*	ī	(as in magazine) *devī*
u	(as in put) Upaniṣad	ū	(as in rude) *mūrti*

dipthongs: e (as in prey) Gaṇeśa; ai (as in aisle) Vaiṣṇava; o as in blow (Govardhan); au (as in now) Gauḍīya

2. The underdotted ṛ is pronounced "ri" as in rich. Kṛṣṇa, Vṛndāvan.

3. Both ś and ṣ may be pronounced "sh." The underdotted ṣ is made with the tip of the tongue slightly curved toward the roof of the mouth. The "c" is pronounced "ch" as in church (*upacāra*).

4. Aspirated consonants (those followed by an "h") are pronounced as follows: bh (as in clubhouse) Bhagavad Gītā; dh (as in roundhouse) Govardhan; th (as in hothouse) Rathyātrā.

5. Underdotted consonants — ṭ, ṭh, ḍ, ḍh, ṇ, and ṣ — are not common phonemes in English and are produced by curling the tongue slightly backward toward the roof of the mouth. The underdotted ḷ is a Tamil phoneme.

6. In Sanskrit, two-syllable words are accented on the first syllable (devī, mū́rti, Viṣṇu). In words of more than two syllables, the penultimate (next to last) syllable is accented if it is long (Gaṇeśa, since "e" is a long vowel; Khajurāho). In such words, if the penultimate is short, then the accent is upon the antipenultimate (third from last) syllable (Himālaya, Dvā́raka, maṅ́ḍala).

7. In the few Hindi words here, there is usually a final syllable (the "a" sound) dropped. Thus, the accent falls on the last syllable in *prasā́d*, and on the first syllable in *darśan* and *āśram*.

APPENDIX III

Glossary

Agni	The Vedic god of fire; also fire itself, especially the sacrificial fire.
āratī	The circling of oil lamp-lights before the image of the deity; used also to describe the entire sequence of honor-offerings made to the deity.
āśram	A forest hermitage; a dwelling place for ascetics, sages, and their students.
āvāhana	"Invoking" a deity to be present at the time of worship. (opp. *visarjana*).
avatāra	The "descent" of a deity upon earth; an incarnation, especially of Viṣṇu.
bali	The type of worship offered to the ancient deities of the *yakṣa* clan, including offerings of flowers, water, incense, as well as meat and liquor.
Bhagavad Gītā	"The Song of the Lord," forms part of the sixth book of the epic Mahābhārata and contains Lord Kṛṣṇa's teaching and revelation to the warrior Arjuna.
Bhāgavata	The name of an early theistic movement which centered around the worship of the Lord (Bhagavān) rather than the rituals of sacrifice.
Bhairava	The "terrible, frightful" one; a fearsome form of Lord Śiva as well as the name for a wider group of ancient deities.
bhakti	"Devotion; honor; love." From *bhaj*, meaning to share, to be devoted, to love. The heart's attitude of devotion and love toward the Lord.
Brahmā	The creator god, having four heads, one to look in each direction. Also known as Prajāpati. Brahmā has no cult.
Brahman	The Supreme Being, the One self-existent power, the Reality which is the source of all being and all knowing.
Brāhmaṇa	The name of the priestly and ritual texts attached to the four Vedas.
brāhmin	The priestly class or a member of the priestly class, charged with the duties of learning, teaching, and performing rites and sacrifices.

daita	Popular Oriya form of *daitya*, one of many class-terms for demons in ancient India, also referring to one of the native non-Aryan tribes. The *daitas* at Purī are, significantly, the servants of Jagannāth — one of their own deities.
darśan	Sanskrit, *darśana*. The "auspicious sight" of the deity. Also a "point of view," or a philosophical position.
devī	"Goddess." Used to refer to the thousands of local goddesses, the consorts of the great gods, and the Great Goddess, the Devī or Mahādevī.
dhām	"Abode, dwelling." A sacred place known to be an "abode" of God. There are four great *dhāms*: Badrināth, Purī, Rāmeśvaram, and Dvārakā.
Durgā	One of the names of the Devī as consort of Śiva. Both a mother and a warrior; her autumn festival Durgā Pūjā is one of North India's great celebrations.
Dvārakā	The *dhām* of West India, located on the coast in Gujerāt. The capital of Lord Kṛṣṇa in his last days and the site of Viṣṇu's Dvārakādhīśa image.
Gaṇeśa	"Lord of Gaṇas." The elephant-headed son of Śiva and Pārvatī and the keeper of the thresholds of space and time, to be honored at the doorway and at the outset of any venture.
Gaṅgā	The sacred river of North India, also personified as a goddess, the daughter of the Himālayas and the sister of Pārvatī.
Gauḍīya	The Bengali sectarian movement of devotion to Kṛṣṇa, launched by Caitanya in the sixteenth century. The Gauḍīyas "rediscovered" the sites of Vraj.
Govardhan	The holy hill of Kṛṣṇa devotion in the Vraj area; the hill said to have been lifted by Kṛṣṇa to protect the villagers from Indra's rains of wrath; the site of the cultus of an ancient local cowherd hero-god.
Gupta	The name of the great North Indian empire from the fourth to sixth century A.D.
Hanumān	The monkey-god, famous as the faithful servant of Rāma who helped Rāma retrieve Sītā from captivity in Laṇkā; worshiped today in his own right as the focus of a vigorous cult.
Indra	The Vedic warrior god, wielder of the thunderbolt and drinker of the intoxicating Soma. In later times, a directional regent.
Jagannāth	"Lord of the Universe." Name of the deity of Purī in Orissa, said to be a manifestation of Kṛṣṇa.
Kālī	The horrific goddess who is both mother of life and destroyer. Sometimes the Śakti of Śiva, and sometimes the supreme being, the Mahādevī, apparently unattached to any consort god.

Kailāsa — The mythical Himālayan mountain said to be the residence of Śiva.

Kāñcī — One of the seven sacred cities of India, situated in the Tamil south.

Kāśī — The "Luminous, Shining" city, one of the seven sacred cities of India on the banks of the Gaṅgā in the north. Also known as Vārāṇasī, or Banāras.

Khajurāho — A temple site built under the patronage of the Chandella kings of north central India in the eleventh century.

Koṇārak — A great Sun temple on the Orissan coast of East India, built in the thirteenth century.

Kṛṣṇa — The ancient cowherd god and hero of India, the adviser of Arjuna on the battlefield of the Mahābhārata war, the playful lover of the milkmaids in Vraj. Said to be an *avatāra* of Viṣṇu, but honored and loved in his own right.

kunkum — Saffron colored powder, used to anoint images of folk deities and used also in ordinary decoration and cosmetics. *Sindūr*, made from red lead, is also used in this way.

Lakṣmī — The goddess who embodies auspiciousness, wealth, and good fortune.

līlā — "Play," especially the play of Kṛṣṇa with his companions and with the milkmaids in Vṛndāvan, where the *līlāsthalas* are the "places of the Lord's play."

liṅga — The "sign, emblem" of Śiva and the focus of Śiva worship.

maṇḍala — The "circle" or circular diagram that functions as a schematic map of the sacred universe. It is the symbolic form of paintings, temples, even cities.

mantra — A sacred formula or utterance; a prayer.

māyā — "Illusion." The illusory quality of this transitory world of "names and forms." The mistaken perception of the world as permanent, when in truth it is a "passage," *saṁsāra*.

melā — A fair, especially a religious fair or festival to which people often come some distance on pilgrimage.

mudrā — In artistic representation, a way of holding the hands and fingers so as to indicate a particular meaning; for example, there is a *mudrā* of protection, a *mudrā* of teaching, a *mudrā* of meditation, and so on.

mūrti — "Form, likeness." The image of the deity, as a focus for worship and *darśan*.

nāga — The ancient serpent deities of India, associated with pools and streams; appropriated by each of the great deities in their rise to supremacy.

Nāthdvārā	The "Lord's Door," a cultic site of the Vallabhites in Rājasthān, where Kṛṣṇa is honored as Śrīnāth-jī.
nāyanmār	The "leaders" (singular, *nāyanār*; plural, *nāyanmār*) of the Tamil Śaiva devotional movement, beginning especially with the three poet-saints who composed the *Tēvāram* between the sixth and the ninth centuries.
nirguṇa	"Without *guṇas*." The *guṇas* are "qualities" or "attributes" and *nirguṇa* refers to that to which no qualities, attributes, or adjectives may be ascribed, i.e. Brahman.
nyāsa	"Placing, marking." The assignment of various deities to different parts of the body, with ritual and prayers.
pādukās	The symbolic "footprints" of a deity or saint, by which the deity or saint is honored.
Pārvatī	"Daughter of the Mountain (*parvat*)." The wife of Śiva, who won the ascetic lord as her husband by austerities.
pīṭha	"Seat, bench." A locus of goddess worship. There are variously said to be 52 or 108 *pīṭhas*.
pralaya	The universal dissolution at the end of one of the vast aeons called a *kalpa*, or a day of Brahmā.
prāṇa	"Breath, life." The life of the deity as established in the image by the *prāṇapratiṣṭhā* rite.
prasād	"Favor, grace." In worship, the food which is offered to the deity and then returned, consecrated, as the "grace" of the Lord to the devotee.
pūjā	"Worship." Ordinarily involves the presentation of "honor offerings" (*upacāras*) to the deity.
pūjārī	The brāhmin priest responsible for the worship (*pūjā*) of the deity.
Purāṇa	One of the eighteen collections of "ancient stories" which preserve traditions of myth, legend, and ritual.
Purī	The *dhām* of the Lord in East India, where the great temple of Kṛṣṇa Jagannāth is located.
Rāma	The virtuous king and hero of the epic Rāmāyana. Said to be an *avatāra* of Viṣṇu, but honored and loved in his own right today. Husband of the faithful wife, Sītā.
Rāmānuja	An eleventh century South India philosopher, who gave a philosophical foundation to the Vaiṣṇava devotional movement which became known as Śrī Vaiṣṇavism.
Rathyātrā	"The Journey of the Chariot." The name of the yearly festival in Purī when the images of Jagannāth, Balarāma, and Subhadrā are taken out in procession in three great chariots.

sādhu	A "holy man," generally an ascetic as well.
saguṇa	"With *guṇas*." The *guṇas* are "qualities " or "attributes" and *saguṇa* refers to that understanding of the divine which is describable with qualities, attributes, and adjectives (opp. *nirguṇa*).
Śaiva	Name for the cult of Śiva and for his followers.
Śākta	Name for the cult of the Devī and for her followers.
śakti	"Energy, power." A term applied to the Goddess, either alone or as the consort of one of the male deities.
śālagrāma	The smooth stone said to be a "natural form" (*svarūpa*) of Viṣṇu.
saṁsāra	"Passage." The term used to describe the ceaseless round of birth and death and rebirth. The changing world.
Śaṅkara	The ca. ninth century teacher (*ācārya*) who is the principal exponent of Non-Dualistic philosophy, called Advaita. Said to have organized Indian ascetics into four orders, with headquarters at the four corners of India.
sannyāsin	"Renouncer." One who has left behind worldly attachments for a life of contemplation, wandering, and asceticism.
śāstra	"Teaching." A sacred treatise or body of learning, such as *Dharmaśāstra*, the "Teachings about Dharma."
Śeṣa	"Remainder." The serpent upon which Viṣṇu reclines on the primordial waters; also called Ananta, the "Endless" one. Śeṣa "remains" even when the universe is destroyed.
śikhara	The spire of a temple, literally the "peak." Also the word for "mountain peak."
śilpaśāstras	The religious treatises having to do with architecture and the arts, the making of temples and images. Intended for *śilpins*, "artists."
Śiva	The "Auspicious One." The many-faced deity, both creator and destroyer, auspicious and seemingly inauspicious, who, along with Viṣṇu and Devī, is one of the three most widely worshiped deities of India.
Skanda	The God of War, son of Śiva and Pārvatī; said to have been raised by six foster-mothers (the Kṛttikās) and therefore is often depicted with six heads and called Kārttikeya.
Śrī Vaiṣṇava	The Viṣṇu *bhakti* movement of South India, which emerged from the line of the Ālvār poet-saints and the philosopher Rāmānuja.
svayambhū	"Self-born, self-manifest." That which is beginningless, uncreated; therefore, used to describe certain images which are said to have appeared spontaneously and were not established by human hands.

tapas "Heat." Especially the heat generated by ascetic practices, believed to be creative, like the brooding heat of a mother hen.

tīrtha "Ford, crossing place." A place of pilgrimage.

tīrthayātrā The journey (*yātrā*) to the sacred place (*tīrtha*). Pilgrimage.

upacāra "Honor offering." A means of showing respect, thus the offerings made to the deity in worship, such as flowers, perfumes, incense, etc.

Upaniṣad One of the speculative sacred texts attached to the four *saṁhitās* (the "collections" of hymns) of the Vedas.

vāhana The "vehicle" upon which a deity rides, usually an animal.

Vaiṣṇava Name for the cult of Viṣṇu and for his followers.

Vallabhite Following the tradition of Vallabha, the fifteenth/sixteenth century philosopher-devotee who gave a philosophical foundation to the rising Kṛṣṇa *bhakti* movement in North India.

Vārāṇasī India's most famous sacred city, one of the seven sacred cities, located on the banks of the Gaṅgā in North India. Also Kāśī, Banāras.

Vārkarī Name of the sectarian devotional movement in Mahārāstra which honors the deity Viṭhobā (a form of Viṣṇu/Kṛṣṇa) in Paṇḍharpur.

Vāstupuruṣa The archetype of a house or temple, personified as a person (*puruṣa*) whose limbs and bodily parts, subdued by the gods, become the symbolic foundation of the temple.

Veda "Wisdom, knowing." Applied to the sacred wisdom of the four Vedic "collections" (*saṁhitās*): The Ṛg, Sāma, Yajur, and Atharva Vedas. More loosely applied to the Brāhmaṇas, Āraṇyakas, and Upaniṣads attached to each collection as well.

visarjana The "dismissal" of the deity after the worship is complete (opp. *āvāhana*).

Viṣṇu Along with Śiva and Devī, one of the three most widely worshiped deities of India. The "Pervader," known for his three great steps by which he claimed the whole universe.

Viśvanāth Śiva, the "Lord of All," as present in the sacred city of Kāśī, Vārāṇasī.

Viṭhobā The deity of Paṇḍharpūr and the focus of Mahārāṣṭrian devotion.

Vraj The homeland of Kṛṣṇa in the Mathurā area of central North India.

Vṛndāvan The village of Vraj especially celebrated as a center of Kṛṣṇa worship, the place of Kṛṣṇa's childhood and youth.

yakṣa/yakṣī	The ancient male and female deities of the "life cult" of non-Aryan India; associated with trees, pools, and vegetative abundance.
yantra	A "device" for harnessing the mind in meditation or worship. A diagram, usually of geometric interlocking triangles and circles.

Index